Classic Children's Games
from Scotland

Kendric Ross

Illustrated by John MacKay

SCOTTISH CHILDREN'S PRESS

First published 1996
SCOTTISH CHILDREN'S PRESS
PO Box 106, Aberdeen AB11 7ZE
Tel: 01224 583777
Fax: 01224 575337

© Kendric Ross 1996
Illustrations © John MacKay 1996
Lettering © Bernadette Main 1996

British Library Cataloguing in Publication Data
A catalogue record for this book is available from the British Library

ISBN: 1 899827 12 9

The rhymes in this book have been collected orally and the author believes
that all are traditional, except where indicated. Reasonable efforts have
beeen made to trace any appropriate copyright holders, but if omissions
have occured the publisher will be pleased to make the necessary correction
in future editions.

Printed and bound in Great Britain by
Cromwell Press, Melksham, Wiltshire

Contents

Editor's Note

AKA – Also Known As

Acknowledgements

Coca-Cola is a registered trademark of
The Coca-Cola Company, and reproduced here
with kind permission of The Coca-Cola Company.

Irn-Bru is a registered trademark. Permission
has been kindly granted by Barr Soft Drinks.

Catch the Train to Glasgow and *I've a laddie in
America* reproduced here with the permission of
The Singing Kettle.

Introduction

I started by asking some friends, 'Do you remember your favourite game at school?'

'Yes,' came the reply, 'It was great, it was called... ah... em... you know that one where we all had a great laugh running about, don't you?'

'No I don't. Which one? There were loads like that.'

'Well, you know, I just can't quite remember, but I'm sure my daughter will know. She played them all too.'

Well it turned out that her daughter fondly remembered playing the games, but couldn't remember exactly how to play them or even what most of them were called.

This is typical, and unless you are a 'superbrain' I'm sure that you're no exception.

Isn't it a real shame? How can you tell your kids about 'that game I loved to play', If you can't remember exactly how to play it?

Don't *your* children deserve to have as much fun as you did?

We all like to reminisce so I invite you to join me In a great nostalgic trip down memory lane.

Public Health Warning

Nowadays, all those pot-bellied, wrinkly, balding, 'health professionals' tell us that our children are 'watching too much telly' and 'playing too many computer games'. In short they don't get enough exercise, and this lack of exercise in our young children will give them heart problems later on in life. So, once you have read this book, STOP! Get out and get started. Become healthy without having to be miserable. These games really are fun to play!

Note to Children

Not everybody grows up to become an Olympic cham-
pion. Let's face it, not everybody wants to be famous and
make loads of money.

However, I promise you, you'll *never* have as much fun
as you can have now. Even some secondary-school children choose to wander aimlessly and boringly about in
groups, all trying to pretend that they are little adults.

Read this book. Try some games. Run and be free while
you can!

If you want to see your mum and dad come alive, show
them this book, ask them which games they played and
say, 'Oh, by the way, can you show me as well?'

Of course, mum and dad were always better at the
game than they can show you now – OF COURSE! I wonder...
were they ever any good?! Stand back and watch them
make a fool of themselves, or maybe, MAYBE, watch that
worried frown disappear and a smile appear on their faces
as they relive their childhood and enjoy having some fun
again. This really is one of the best ways to have good
healthy exercise and have fun at the same time.

Note to Parents

Come on big yins. You and I know fair well that we all go
about our business acting responsibly, setting a good
example, being very serious, and outwardly showing that
aura of adulthood. However you and I know that underneath that cold exterior we are after all, children at heart.
I wrote this book for parents, grandparents and teachers
as well, so that you too can have a long trip down
memory lane; ask your neighbour, your workmate, everyone you meet, 'Do you remember such-and-such game?'
and watch the expression on their faces.

I started to write rough notes on these games from my own experience, then added that of friends, before I researched other books, and it was quite amazing what a chord this struck with everyone; to have these people recall a game and then trying not to burst out laughing from watching their inept demonstration, 'This is how we did it.' Equally, I was amazed at how little people could remember, so I thought it was high time that something was done about it. These games are far too good to be allowed to die out, so I set about the task of writing this book in what I hope you will find to be a very reader-friendly form, giving you all the information you need without going completely over the top. When I looked at other supposed 'children's books', I found them to be written by adults who apparently had never tried half of the games, had added contrived variants of impossible games, or if you didn't know the game then the book didn't tell you enough so that you could play it. At the other extreme I found myself on information overload; some dry and academic authors had compiled a virtual encyclopaedia on some children's games.

I do admit to a certain bias; a Scottish bias. I hope that I have managed to put in a fair smattering of Scots words and phrases without overdoing it; just enough to help keep our language and culture alive, but at the same time the reader should have little difficulty in following the text. If you do come up against a word you don't know, just look up the Glossary at the end of this book on page 119.

Finally, if you are demonstrating any of these games to your children, remember that you're not as young as you used to be, and probably not as fit as you think you are. It's especially important to limber up and stretch your muscles before running about daft! Don't show off too much either; your kid might just turn out to be a whole lot better than you are. Be sure not to get injured as there's currently something like a ten year waiting list to see a physiotherapist on the NHS, and more than likely 20 years if you are foolish enough to admit to how you got your injury.

Go to it, and most of all enjoy the games. As the older kids say nowadays, 'GET A LIFE!'

The Games Selected

I have selected games that I feel are viable – the classic children's games that have stood the test of time and are still just as enjoyable today. There was little or no point in writing about the *Cleek and Gird* as there aren't many blacksmiths about and even if you had the right gear it isn't safe any more as there are far too many cars on the roads. Who wants to make a 'Bogey', 'Guider' or 'Kairtie' – fine but they don't make prams like they used to, do they? It's a non-starter unless you can find two good pairs of wheels. Maybe there is a bit of truth in the belief that, 'things aren't as good as they used to be' after all!

It's impossible to play any games without some slight risk. It often seems that the higher the risk, the more fun the game, or if there isn't some element of risk then the children simply aren't interested. Some of the games that I remember playing like *Knuckles* and *Dead Man's Fall* have been positively excluded because they are dangerous and probably best forgotten.

It must also be remembered that because these are children's games and often passed on by word of mouth they have tended to evolve over the years either because the children found a better way to play – which meant that the game was adapted to what they had available and to suit their own circumstances – or someone simply misheard the 'instructor'. We've all heard of the game

4

Chinese Whispers – how else could you get the names *Bar the Door* and *Barley Door* to describe the same game?

So please remember, there are no hard and fast rules as such; if the game isn't quite how you played it, or want to play it, then change it to suit yourself.

I do have two further rules that you really do need to go by:

1. Do not spoil your playground games with too many silly and petty rules.
2. The most important rule of all is to *enjoy* your games.

Tick ~ Tack

1 *How to Start a Game – Choosing IT*

AKA: On; He; Het; Mannie

The person who is chosen to start a game, or play the lead role, is called many different names depending on what part of the country they live in. Throughout this book the term **IT** has been used. In Scots we say 'Wha's het?' meaning, 'Who is **IT**?'

There are many traditional methods of choosing who is to be **IT**.

Choosing Between Two People or Two Teams

Tossing a Coin

Action
A coin is tossed by one player and the other shouts out either 'heads' or 'tails'. If 'the other' calls correctly, this person can decide whether or not he wishes to start, or whether he wishes to make his opponent start. This is still the most common way to start a football or rugby match. However, be very careful not to agree to some trickery like, 'Heads I win, tails you lose!'

Tick-Tack

AKA: Tickum-Tackum
Action
The two opponents, or team captains, move apart by several paces, then either one of them shouts 'Tick-Tack' to signal that they turn around and walk in a straight line towards one another, heel hard in front of toe. They each

take steps turn about until finally the one who ends up with no room to 'heel-toe' without touching their opponent's foot is the loser. The other player therefore becomes **IT**. It is customary for one person to shout 'Tick', and the other 'Tack', with every step that they each take.

Variation
Step 'toe in front of toe' with knees and foot twisted inwards.

Jumps

AKA: Jumpies

Action
Similar to *Tick-Tack* but this time the opponents jump towards each other with their feet together, taking turn about. Whoever can manage a jump that lands on his opponent's feet wins and becomes **IT**.

Choosing from a Small Group of People

AKA: Dipping

Counting out can be used for choosing between two people, but is more commonly used as a sort of ritual in choosing who is to be **IT** from a group, repeating a rhyme until there is only one person remaining. The rhyme used is called a 'dip'. At the end of this process the person left in becomes **IT**. Elsewhere, someone may be 'chappit oot', which literally means 'knocked out'.

Having decided on what game you are going to play, the person who will recite the counting out rhyme is the first to yell 'Bags **IT**!' Several people usually yell out at nearly the same time but there is always one just that split second ahead of the others that the group can identify. This person becomes the 'rhymer'.

One Potato...
Rhyme
One potato, two potato, three potato, four,
Five potato, six potato, seven potato, MORE.
Action

T	T	T	T
One potato	two potato	three potato	four
Five potato	six potato	seven potato	MORE

T – tap

The person elected to recite the rhyme calls 'spuds up' and everyone gathers round in a circle with clenched fists held out as if grasping a vertical rope in each hand. Each fist is a spud! As the rhyme is chanted, the rhymer taps his counting spud on top of each of the spuds in the circle, until on the eighth tap he reaches the word 'more' and stops at that spud. Every time the rhymer (or 'spudder') reaches the word 'more' then that spud is out and has to go behind the player's back. The rhymer has to keep one hand in and has to remember to count the counting hand as well by 'spudding' right fist over left and left fist over right. When both single hands are out then both hands are clasped together and held forward as one 'spud' until the player is finally counted out for good and keeps both hands behind their back until the person with the last hand in is chosen as **IT**.

This particular 'dip' is very laborious and it can take so long that there is often little or no time left to play the chosen game. As such, it is almost a game in itself!

One Potato........

Choosing from a Large Group of People

Twenty-One Counts Your Man

For very large groups such as a whole class this is a very quick and fair method of deciding who will be **IT**.

Action

The person counting says, 'Twenty-one counts your man. One, two, three, four...', all the way up to the number 21, tapping each person with each word of the rhyme. The group stands or sits in a circle with one foot inward and the person on whose foot the number 21 lands becomes **IT**.

Sky Blue

Rhyme

One, two, sky blue,
All out but you!

Action

This is another quick way to choose **IT** from a large group of people, with the counter tapping each person with each word of the rhyme. The person who is tapped with the word 'you' is **IT**.

Eeny, Meeny...

Rhymes

Version A:

Eeny, meeny, miney, mo,
Catch a tigger by the toe,
If he squeals let him go,
Eeny, meeny, miney, mo,
You are OUT.

Version B:

Eeny, meeny, miney, mo,
Sit the baby on the po,
When it's done, wipe its bum,
Stick the paper up the LUM.

Action

T	T	T	T
Eeny	meeny	miney	mo
Catch	a tigger	by the	toe
If he	squeals	let him	go
Eeny	meeny	miney	mo
You	are	OUT	

T – Tap

The counting is often done by pointing to, or touching, each person with each word in the rhyme. Sometimes everyone can put a foot into the centre instead. Every time the last word of the rhyme lands on someone, they are out. This continues until there is only one person left.

Oor Wee Jeanie

Rhyme

Oor wee Jeanie has a nice clean peeny,
So guess what colour it is.

Action

Whoever gets the tap with the word 'is' shouts out any colour they wish to choose, and that colour is then spelt and counted out, for example: B–L–U–E. Whoever the last letter lands on is out.

This method of selection allows for some mischief, as it is not very difficult to quickly count a word in your head, so that you deliberately put someone out for the remainder of the count.

I think, I think

Rhyme
I think, I think, I smell a stink,
Coming from Y-O-U.

Action
This rhyme never ceases to amuse. Each person is tapped with each word of the rhyme and not only does the person who is tapped with 'U' get put out, but they also have the added indignity of being accused of smelling!

2   Chasing and Catching Games

All over the world children play different kinds of chasing games. Very often the children being chased will chant a teasing rhyme like:

Ha, ha, ha; he, he, he;
You can't catch me for a wee bawbee.

Sometimes the word 'bawbee' becomes 'bumbee'.

Chasing Games

Tig

AKA: Tag; Chasie; Touch; He; It

Rhyme

Eeny, meeny, miney, mo,
Catch a tigger by the toe,
If he squeals, let him go,
Eeny, meeny, miney, mo,
You are **IT**!

In this rhyme, the word 'out' has been replaced by **IT**, so it is really a case of counting in rather than counting someone out.

Action

In *Tig*, the person chosen to be **IT** (using the rhyme to establish this), has to chase the others, who all run away from him. When he touches or 'tags' someone, the chaser shouts out, 'Tag you're **IT**!' so the person who has been tagged then becomes the chaser.

In order to save any confusion, the person who has just been tagged should shout, 'I'm **IT**!', or 'I'm **HE**!' so that the others are certain as to who is about to chase them, otherwise it really can be confusing in a cramped and noisy playground.

Levoy

AKA: Reliev-O; Leavey; Leroy
Action
Levoy is one of the more sophisticated forms of *Tig* and quite similar to the *Buzz-Off* form of Hide-and-Seek (see Chapter 3).

Choose someone to be a catcher; or choose two catchers if more than six people are playing. The catcher/catchers start from the den, a circle chalked on the ground, or a certain agreed area into which all of those captured will be escorted and held in custody. Everyone scatters out, and the catchers leave the den to try to catch them. As each runner is caught, usually by physically holding them for a count of three, or sometimes by the 'head and tail' method (tag on both the head and bottom), they are put into the den. However, the sport is that an 'outie' (that is someone who is still free) can sneak up and rush into the den shouting, 'Levoy all free!', 'Ha la Levoy!', or something similar, so that all of those held prisoner in the den are released and allowed to run free again. The game finishes when all of the outies have been captured.

Hospital Tig

AKA: French Touch; Wounded Tiggy; Poison Tiggy
Action
Choose someone to be a catcher; the rest then run away. When someone gets caught he has to hold on to the part of the body on which he was tagged when he becomes

Hospital Tig

the chaser. This can be on the head, leg, foot or any other part of the body, and needless to say, it can be absolutely hilarious for those watching a chaser struggling with such an impediment. For example, if you have been touched on the foot you have to hop after the others while holding on to that foot.

This game is better played in a reasonably confined space such as a very large room, or in an alcove in the playground. This will give the chaser a better chance of catching someone or otherwise he is likely to become fair scunnered. This game is that wee bit more interesting as the chaser is not just trying to catch someone by tagging them anywhere, but is also trying to touch them in a particular spot that will be amusing to his friends.

Tunnel Tig

AKA: Underarm Tig; Underground Tig; Scarecrow Tig

This is a team game of chase and and is excellent for giving the participants an appreciation of the importance of co-operation and teamwork, and also helps in developing tactical skills.

Action

Depending on the number of participants, two to four people are chosen to be the 'chasers' and 'guards' and the rest become the 'runners'. When someone is tagged they must stand up against a particular wall with one arm outstretched, so that when several runners have been caught they form an imaginary tunnel. The runners who are still free try to run underneath the outstretched arms of those that have been caught and shout 'You're free', so that they can escape and run away again. It is therefore tactical for the chasers to have at least one guard near the tunnel to try to prevent people from being freed. Runners might go close enough to a guard to tempt that

Tunnel Tig

guard out of position (by chasing them), so that another runner can slip past and set someone free again. It is customary for those who have been caught to try to make the tunnel as long as possible so that the tunnel is more difficult for the chasers to guard.

Variations

Both arms are held against the wall, or a leg is propped against the wall.

However, if there is no suitable wall available this game is called *Underground Tig* or *Scarecrow Tig.* When you are tagged you stay at the spot where you were caught and stand with your legs astride. You can be freed again if one of your side dashes over and jouks through your legs.

Chain Tig

AKA: Chainie; Chain He; Nets; Link Tig

Action

A chaser is chosen and once someone has been caught they hold hands. The chase begins again, and continues until a long chain of children is formed. Only those at each end of the chain are allowed to tag and so catch those being chased. No-one can be caught when there is a break in the chain. It can be great fun indeed with many children in the chain chasing only the few that remain free and because the middle parts of the chain are not allowed to catch them, they can escape under the arms of those in the middle; remember it is only those at the ends of the chain that are allowed to tag someone! Last caught is the winner and sometimes, to celebrate, the chain forms a 'V' shape and the winner runs into the narrow part to end the game. The winner becomes **IT** for the next game.

Mr Wolf

Action

Someone is chosen to be Mr Wolf. Pick a home, den, or any safe place where the wolf cannot harm the rest of the group, for instance a large circle chalked on to the ground, or any line that the wolf is not allowed to cross. Mr Wolf starts walking away from the den with the other children following and calling out: 'What's the time, Mr Wolf?'

Mr Wolf does not turn round but instead keeps on walking and in a very gruff voice replies: 'Half past two', or any time that he can think of.

The children keep asking and the wolf keeps replying, all the time luring them further and further away from the den until suddenly the wolf replies, 'DINNER TIME!'

The wolf spins round and chases them as they scream and shout in a mock state of panic and rush back to the safety of the den. If Mr Wolf catches anyone before they reach the den, then he will be Mr Wolf for the next game.

The Hound and Hares

Action

One player from the group is chosen to be **IT**, or the hound that starts the game off. The remaining players are all hares. All but one of the hares spread out and lay a jersey or blazer on the ground to mark areas (forms) where they will be safe. The hares squat down by these bases; the hare without a form stands fairly close to the hound.

The hound shouts, 'Go hare; go!' and the loose hare runs off with the hound in hot pursuit. If the loose hare gets tired of being chased and tags one of the other hares, he can take over the safety of the form and the tagged hare has to run off or risk being caught by the hound. If the hound tags this new loose hare they swap places, so that the hare becomes the hound, and so the game continues until usually everyone becomes too exhausted or wants to play something else.

This is a particularly fast moving chasing game, and is well suited to older children and agile adults.

There are of course many other chasing games played world-wide. Perhaps you know some more games, or call some of these games by a different name.

Catching Games

Red Rover

Action
Two captains are elected and they each pick players turn about for their teams. A team size of about four to six players on each side is ideal, although it is possible to play with larger groups. One of the teams elects to go first. The teams assemble with hands joined to form two chains along opposite lines. (It should be remembered that this was originally a street game played from one pavement to another so the lines should not be too far apart.) The 'starting' team go into a very serious whispered conversation about who they should choose, and this decided they chant, 'Red Rover, Red Rover, we want Jill over', normally choosing the weakest in the opposite team. Jill's team chants, 'Break it, break it, break it, BREAK IT!' as Jill comes running over and charges at the opposite chain. Jill uses her speed and weight to try and break open one of the links in the chain by forcing their hands apart, and if she is successful in breaking through the chain, she goes back to re-join her own team, but if she

Red Rover

fails she has to join the other team.

When it is Jill's team's turn again, they have two options: they can call as before, 'Red Rover...' and challenge one of the players from the opposition, or if they would rather have Jill back, they can chant, 'Tick, tack, tick, tack, we want Jill back', to which the other team chants, 'Don't break it, don't break it, don't break it, DON'T BREAK IT'. Jill has to try to get through her original chain without breaking it, perhaps with a sudden jouk under a gap in the chain. If she does get by she rejoins her original team.

The game is over when only one person is left at the other side or, if you are playing at school, the winning side is the one with the most players in their team when the bell goes.

Bar the Door

AKA: Barley Door; Barley; Burrie; Joukie; Dodgie

Action

This is another fast moving game in which the skills of jinkin' together with a little bit of pace combine to help you to succeed. Someone is chosen as the catcher to stand in the middle between two lines such as opposite sides of a pitch. (If there are no lines, you can run between two dens instead.) The catcher calls out a player's name and that person has to try and jink past the catcher to reach the other side. The players at the line or den will chant: 'Get caught, get caught, GET CAUGHT'. If he reaches the other line without being tagged he shouts, 'Bar the door' (or barley door) which is the cue for all the others to rush to the same side, being careful not to be tagged by the catcher of course. Those caught also become catchers so that the number of catchers increases and it becomes more and more difficult to cross over safely, especially as the catchers close in on their target with very loud chants of, '10, 9, 8, 7, 6, 5, 4, 3, 2, 1, ZERO!' in the hope that this will panic them into being caught. Very often everyone joins in this chant. The person who was last caught claims the right to call out someone's name, and in the version called 'Barley' the person who is caught must say 'Barley, one, two, three' before he is allowed to choose someone to run at him. It would not be the same at all without all these little rituals which have to be performed!

The whole process is repeated time and time again until the last person to remain free is the winner and becomes **IT** for the next game.

British Bulldogs

Action
One person is chosen to be the 'Bulldog' (the catcher) before the start of the game. Everyone else assembles on one side of a pitch or at a playground wall, and when the Bulldog shouts 'British Bulldogs' they all have to run to the other side of the pitch or a certain line without being caught. Just to make sure that everyone is paying attention, the Bulldog will occasionally shout something silly like 'French Poodles' in which case everyone stays where they are. To catch someone they must be physically restrained and lifted up off the ground to the count 'One, two, three, British Bulldogs'. Other methods of catching include being 'head and tailed', tapped three times on the back, or dragged to a boundary. Unless the catching procedure is fully enacted you can struggle free and escape. It is customary to start off by trying to catch the smaller children first as they are easier to hold and will help you to catch the bigger ones later on.

Any players who are caught during each run also become catchers. The last remaining player still free at the end is the winner, but with so many catchers 'bulldogging' people at the same time, it can be difficult to decide who was last caught. In the event of a dispute between two players a toss of a coin will resolve this.

Be prepared for a few bruises if you play this game!

Boatman

AKA: Mr Farmer; Farmer Farmer

Action

Someone is chosen as the Boatman and stands in between the sides of a pitch, or two chosen lines. Everyone else stands along one line and chants, 'Boatman, boatman, may we cross the river?' and the boatman replies, 'You can't cross the river, unless you're wearing red' (or whatever colour the boatman chooses).

Those who are wearing red show what they are wearing and are allowed to cross safely. Even a tiny fleck of colour in a jersey will do! Sometimes the boatman will have a bit of fun and delay the proceedings by saying in a deep voice, 'The river's far too fast, and you'll DROWN!' The boatman keeps calling out different colours until all but one has been eliminated from the game and the winner becomes the boatman for the next game. If you do not have the colour you are out.

Variation

Another version allows those wearing the colour to cross safely, but those who are not are given a second chance and have to try to jink past the boatman without being tagged. If someone is tagged, he joins the boatman in the middle and becomes another catcher, so as the game progresses it becomes more and more difficult to cross the river. The best chance of winning is to be wearing lots of different colours.

The word Boatman in the chant may be changed to Mr Farmer, Crocodile, or whatever the children decide.

The Train

Action

This is a very simple, traditional playground game in which a few children decide to start a train by holding on to the waist of the person in front. They shout chants and encourage others to 'come and join the train', as they trot past weaving side to side and round in big circles.

A train running through the middle of someone else's game seems to be well tolerated by the schoolchildren, and those who are bored with their own game join in anyway. Those joining the train simply catch hold of the waist of the last person in the train and follow on behind.

The Train

Can you imagine what a laugh it would be if most of the children in your school playground left their own games and joined the train to weave in and out of the playground, and round and round the school? Would you have enough children to stretch right around the school? It does happen!

When the train is thought to be long enough, the 'driver' at the front tries to catch the 'guard' at the end to finish the game.

A Song – Catch the Train to Glasgow

Here is the train to Glasgow.
And here is the driver Mr MacIvor, that drove the train to
        Glasgow.
And here is the guard from Donniebristle,
who waved his flag and blew his whistle,
to tell the driver Mr MacIvor,
to start the train to Glasgow.
And here is a boy called Donald MacBrayne,
who came to the station to catch the train.
And saw the guard from Donniebristle,
wave his flag and blow his whistle,
to tell the driver Mr MacIvor,
to start the train to Glasgow.

And here is the guard a kindly man,
who at the last minute hauled into the van,
that fortunate boy called Donald MacBrayne,
who came to the station to catch the train.
And saw the guard from Donniebristle,
wave his flag and blow his whistle,
to tell the driver Mr MacIvor,
to start the train to Glasgow.

And here are the hens, and here are the cocks,
cluckin' and crowing inside a box,
In charge of the guard that kindly man,
who at the last minute hauled into the van,
that fortunate boy called Donald MacBrayne,
who came to the station to catch the train.
And saw the guard from Donniebristle,
wave his flag and blow his whistle,
to tell the driver Mr MacIvor,
to start the train to Glasgow.

And here is the train which gave a jolt,
and loosened the catch and loosened the bolt.
Let out the hens and let out the cocks,
cluckin' and crowing out of their box.
In charge of the guard that kindly man,
who at the last minute hauled into the van,
that fortunate boy called Donald MacBrayne
who came to the station to catch the train.
And saw the guard from Donniebristle,
wave his flag and blow his whistle,
to tell the driver Mr MacIvor,
to start the train to Glasgow.

The guard chased a hen and missing it fell,
the hens were cluckin', the cock as well.
Unless you were there, you haven't a notion,
the flurry, the fuss, the noise, the commotion.
Caused by the train, that gave a jolt,
and loosened the catch and loosened the bolt.
Let out the hens and let out the cocks,
cluckin' and crowing out of their box.
In charge of the guard that kindly man,
who at the last minute hauled into the van,
that fortunate boy called Donald MacBrayne

who came to the station to catch the train.
And saw the guard from Donniebristle,
wave his flag and blow his whistle.
To tell the driver Mr MacIvor,
to start the train to Glasgow.

Now Donald was quick and Donald was neat,
And Donald was nimble on his feet,
He caught the hens and he caught the cocks,
and he put them back in their great big box,
The guard was pleased, as pleased could be,
he invited Donald to come to tea,
on Saturday at Donniebristle,
and he'd let him blow his lovely whistle.
He said in all his life he'd never,
seen a boy so quick and clever.
And so did the driver Mr MacIvor,
that drove the train to Glasgow.

Written by W. Horsbrugh
Composed by P. Trezise
© Singing Kettle

3 Hiding, Seeking and Hunting Games

The original games of hiding, seeking and hunting are many centuries old and form a part of our natural development into adults. It is a basic instinct to learn hunting and seeking skills as we grow up, just like a little kitten plays with a dead leaf as if it were a real mouse. Hiding could save us from real danger, and we all have an instinctive need to hone these survival skills which could have protected us in the wild many centuries ago. In modern society we have progressed from hunting for food, to farming for food, then into an industrial nation in which people work to earn money with which they buy food. We do not quite need the same level of these survival skills nowadays, but the instinct is still very strong, so we still like to practise them, much like a well-fed domestic cat will still hunt and kill mice or birds just for the sport.

In all of the versions of *Hide-and-Seek* described here, a particular spot such as a lamp post or tree is used as the 'block', and a doorway or circle marked on the ground is used for a 'den'. All of the games start with the seeker making a 'count'. The count is up to whichever number in whatever manner that everyone agrees upon. For example, it could be 'count up to 50 in ones', or 'up to 100 in tens'. The block, or den, can also be called *home, dell* or *dellie.*

In this chapter, emphasis has been placed on games that are popular or more interesting and are mostly of the racing home variety.

Hide and Seek

Some Hide-and-Seek Rhymes

In the basic form of *Hide-and-Seek* in which there is no den or block, and the hider is simply found, the 'outie' who has just been caught will often call out a warning rhyme to let the others know that he has been caught. They stay well hidden if his voice sounds nearby with words like, 'Stay in, stay in, wherever you are, the monkey's oot o' the Jeely Jar!' Likewise, if for some other reason the game becomes a 'bogie', or 'whitewash', the seeker may shout, 'Come oot, come oot, wherever you be, the monkey's up the apple tree', or, 'Come oot, come oot, wherever you are, the game's up the pole', or, 'Come oot, come oot, wherever you are, the game's a bogie'. All of these are commonly used expressions.

Draw the Snake

This is a ritual used as the elaborate start for a game of *Hide-and-Seek*.

Action

The person who is **IT** stands with his back to the group, leaning, face hidden in forearm, against a wall or post, to prevent him from being able to see. Someone from the group assumes leadership, steps forward and draws a squiggly snake all the way down the person's back with their finger, and chants in a gruff voice, 'I draw a snake upon your back, who will put in the eye?' The leader steps back and another child from the group steps forward and pokes the person near the top of their back then steps back to re-join the group. This ritual completed, **IT** turns around and has to guess who poked him and at the same time sets a task like, 'Run once round the school and count up to fifty'. If he guesses correctly which person poked in the eye, that person has to carry out the task set as the group skedaddles into hiding. The 'poker' therefore becomes the seeker and the game of *Hide-and-Seek* starts.

However, if **IT** is wrong then he must do the task himself! This procedure continues until **IT** guesses correctly so that the game can start.

Block – All Hide, One Seek

AKA: Blocky; Block: one, two, three.

This is by far and away the most common version played throughout Britain.

Action

A player is chosen to be **IT**, or the 'seeker'. A tree or lamp-post is used as the block and the seeker leans towards it, burying his face into his right forearm just to be sure that he cannot keek out and see where someone is

Draw The Snake

trying to hide. He counts out loud up to an agreed number, keeping his eyes shut, while the rest of the group run off to hide. The count is often made in fives or tens such as 5, 10, 15, 20... all the way up to 100, and on reaching this the seeker yells out, 'Here I come, ready or not!' The seeker then sets off from the block to search for his play-mates, and if he spots someone he shouts out their name and they race each other back to the block. If the seeker wins this race he will shout, 'One, two, three, block, block, block!' and he bangs his fist with each word as he strikes the block. However, if the 'outie' manages to beat the seeker back to the den, then he is allowed to run off and hide again so that the seeker has to count all over again. The first person 'blocked' will become the seeker for the next game. Once all of the players have been blocked or freed themselves the game is over.

Sometimes, a few of the players can swap items of clothing then deliberately show just a little bit of a distinctive jersey sleeve or trouser leg so that the seeker is tricked into calling out the wrong name. He may rush back to the den and block the wrong person by mistake. In this event the seeker has to count all over again and the outie stays free. This can add interest to the game and indeed a great deal of confusion.

Buzz Off – All Hide, Two Seek

Action

The same rules as *Block* apply here, with one added rule that any outie still free is allowed to sneak up and rush into the den shouting 'Buzz off' so that all of the prisoners in the den are freed again. (A den is used instead of a block.) It can be very frustrating for the seeker to have to start all over again. If the others are agreeable, it is sometimes better to allow two seekers like in the chasing game of *Levoy* (see Chapter 2); that way someone can guard the den.

Man Hunt – All Seek, One Hide

Action
Someone is chosen as **IT** and becomes the only one to go off and hide and, after the count, the rest of the children go off to search for the hidden one. First person to find him and call out his name becomes **IT** for the next game.

Variation
The hider can try to sneak back to the den without being captured, and if seen he races the others back to the den. If he succeeds in getting there first, he is allowed to go off and hide again.

Sardines

Action
If a suitable spot can be found that has lots of large hiding places then *Man Hunt* can be modified to become *Sardines*. The game is often played around a house and garden that has lots of nooks and crannies. As each player finds the hider they try to sneak in beside him without any of the others noticing. This continues until only one person is left searching. The first one to find the sardine become **IT** for the next game. You can get rather squashed up during this game, hence the name *Sardines*.

Multiplication Touch

AKA: One Man Plus

Action
This game starts off with one seeker and as the hiders

become found they join him as seekers, spreading out in search of the rest until they are all found. There is nothing more boring than being out of a game and waiting for it to end, so when the hiders become seekers it keeps their interest in the game. In some areas, just being seen by a seeker is not enough, and local variations exist where, for example, the outie must be caught and held for a count of ten. This is an example of a seeking game that has no den or block.

Kick the Can

This game is sheer magic. If you have never played it, be sure to try it now. Alongside *Block* it is one of the most popular forms of Hiding and Seeking.

Action

A tin can, or sometimes a wooden block, is placed in the den. (If a wooden block is used the game is called *Kick the Block*.) A player is chosen to be **IT**, or the 'den-keeper'. One of the hiders gives the can an almighty boot away from the den so that the den-keeper has to retrieve the can back to the den before he can start the count. This time some outies may stay as close as possible to the den without being seen. If the den-keeper sees someone hiding he shouts out their name and they race each other back to the can. The outie stays free if he wins the race. However, if the den-keeper wins the race, he grabs the can and dunts it three times on the ground, so that the outie is captured and becomes a prisoner in the den.

The prisoners can be freed if an outie runs up to the den, kicks the can well out of the den, and shouts, 'It's kicked by me, and you're all free'. The poor den-keeper has to replace the can in the den and count all over again while all of those freed run off to hide.

However, it is just as likely that the den-keeper will spot

Kick The Can

someone attempting a rescue and catch them instead. As the name 'den-keeper' suggests, he tends to be a bit canny and not stray too far from the den.

This game is particularly interesting because the den-keeper has to guard the den as well as go seeking, and there is of course the added excitement of hearing the clatter of a noisy can. If the den-keeper is being over cautious in guarding the den, his prisoners inside the den may taunt him with a chant like, 'Gaun oot, gaun oot, ya lazy hen, an' look fur a' yer choockies'.

Hunt the Keg

Action

Two teams are selected, one to be the 'coastguards' and one to be the 'smugglers'. The coastguards have to protect their den from infiltration by the smugglers. The 'keg', which in olden days would have contained whisky for real adult smugglers, is any distinctive, small object that can easily be held fully enclosed in a someone's hand. It might be a coloured marble, rubber or pencil sharpener.

After the usual count, the smugglers run off into hiding, and then try to sneak the keg back home to the den to win the game. The smugglers can change who holds the keg during the course of the game, and it does not matter how many smugglers the coastguards catch and detain in their prison (the prison is a separate spot from the den for this game): so long as one smuggler manages to reach the den with the keg, the smugglers win. If a coastguard catches a smuggler and shouts, 'Stand and deliver', and that smuggler opens his hand to reveal the keg, then the coastguards have won. The winning side becomes the smugglers in the next game.

Much guile is employed as some smugglers may deliberately show themselves as decoys, pretend to hold the keg, and pretend they are shocked at being caught, all in the hope that the real 'kegger' can sneak home to the den; true teamwork indeed.

Queenie

4 *Ball Games*

When you are playing any ball games near windows, make sure that you use a sponge ball or a hollow rubber ball to avoid causing any damage.

Queenie

AKA: Ali Baba

Rhymes

Version A

Queenie, Queenie, who's got the ball,
Is she big, or is she small,
Is she fat, or is she thin,
Or does she have a double chin?

Version B

Ali Baba, Ali Baba,
Who's got the ball?
I ain't got it, in my pocket,
So Ali Baba, Ali Baba,
Who's got the ball?

Action

Someone is chosen to be **IT**, or 'queenie', and stands to face a wall, or simply with her back to the others who stand about four or five steps behind her. Queenie throws a ball, such as a tennis ball, backwards over her shoulder, or upwards from in between her legs, and the players scramble to try to catch the ball before it hits the ground. If anyone manages, they shout 'caught ball', and this girl becomes Queenie for the next game. More often than not, the ball touches the ground so that the first player to grab it, picks it up and hides it behind her back. They all form a row and all pretend to have the ball. Someone shouts 'Ready' to let Queenie know to turn round and guess who has the ball, or one of the rhymes can be chanted.

Queenie then tries to determine who has it by saying: 'Jeanie jump up', 'Annie do a hauf birl', etc. Finally if Queenie guesses correctly she goes again, but if she is wrong then the girl with the ball takes over as Queenie.

Bouncy/Stotty

Rhyme
One, two, three, a-leerie,
Four, five, six, a-leerie,
Seven, eight, nine, a-leerie,
Ten, a-leerie postman.

  all numbers – bounce/stot
  a – lift leg
  lee – bounce under leg
  rie – leg down

Action
This is a game for one person, played with a bouncy ball. An old tennis ball or rubber ball of the same size is ideal.

As you sing the rhyme, the ball is stotted with each number and every time you sing, 'a-leerie', you step over the bouncing ball by lifting one of your legs over it. When you reach the word 'postman' at the end you birl around then catch the ball to end the game.

Plainie, Clappie

Rhyme

	Actions
Plainie, clappie,	Throw, clap.
Roll-a-pin, tebaccy,	Roll arms.

Plainie Clappie

Right hand, left hand,	Throw from right, then left hand.
Through you go,	Throw ball up-and-under through leg.
Big Burly O.	Turn right around, catch ball and
	stop, or continue.

Action

This is a game which can be played solo, or against others to see who can get the highest score. In its simplest form only one tennis-size ball is used, but as you become more skilled you can progress to two balls. If you are a whizz kid and can manage three balls, perhaps you should consider joining a circus!

Face a fairly smooth wall, throw the ball onto the wall and catch the rebound before it hits the ground. Every time you manage to finish the rhyme with all the actions correct you score a point. When you drop the ball you are out, and it is the next player's turn.

Variation

Depending on your skill level, the players can decide at the start of the game to use two balls. If two balls are used the game is often called *Doubles,* or *Doublers.* Three balls is called *Throublers.*

An alternative longer rhyme would be:

Plainie, clappie,
Roond-yer-back and backie,
Right hand, left hand,
Birl aroond and cradly, *
Through the right leg,
Through the left leg,
Touch the grund,
An' roll the baccy.

* with each completed verse exchange the word *cradly* for another word asterisked below.

Actions used
plainie – throw ball against the wall and catch the rebound

clappie – clap your hands together

roond-yer-back – transfer ball, one hand to the other, behind your back

backie – throw ball backwards and overhead

right (left) hand – catch the ball in your right (left) hand

*cradly – cradle arms rocking sideways as if cradling a baby

*double clappie – clap twice

*Roll-a-pin (or rolly) – roll forearms in circular paddling motion

*oxter breestie – cross arms over chest, touch breasts, then catch the ball

*heel, *knee, *hip, *cheek – touch these parts

Oliver Twist

Rhyme

Oliver Twist, can you do this?
If so, do so.
Number one, touch your tongue,
Number two, touch your shoe,
Number three, touch your knee,
Number four, touch the floor,
Number five, take a dive,
Number six, pick up sticks,
Number seven, fly to heaven,
Number eight, shut the gate,
Number nine, drink some wine,
Number ten, begin again.

Action

The ball is thrown against a wall and the various actions are done in between catches while the ball is still in the air.

The actions really are self explanatory, so it is left up to the individual as to how elaborate they wish to make them.

Variation

Perhaps before trying the full version of *Oliver Twist* you might like to try the shorter version which is common in central Scotland:

Oliver Twist you can't do this,
So what's the use in trying,
If so touch your toe,
Clap your hands,
And through below. (Between legs.)

Post Box

Rhyme
The pillar box is fat and red,
Its mouth is very wide,
I'm going to get some letters,
and pop them all inside.
1, 2, 3, 4, 5, 6, 7, 8, 9, 10.

Action
This rhyme can be used for either throwing a ball against the wall, or just a game of *stotty*.

Over the Rainbow

This is a deceptively difficult game as it is hard to see the ball when someone else has just jumped over it.

Action
Everyone queues up one behind the other in a line, facing a wall. The first person throws the ball against the wall, shouts a colour of the rainbow and, as the ball bounces back, he jumps legs astride over the ball and the next person in the line catches it. He then shouts another

colour of the rainbow, jumps over the ball, and joins the first person at the back of the line.

If anyone fails to catch the ball they lose their shot and have to go to the back so that the turn goes to the next person.

If you have any bother remembering the colours of the rainbow, imagine a strange person called ROY G. BIV. This gives you the first letters of all the colours: Red, Orange, Yellow... and so on. Can you guess the rest?

Wounded, Dying, Dead

AKA: Three Lives; Cat's Lives

Action

For this game it is safer to use a relatively soft ball.

Start off this game by forming a circle with all the player's legs astride and feet touching. The ball is then thrown vertically upwards and allowed to bounce inside the circle. When the ball runs through someone's legs, everyone dashes for safety as the object of the game is for this player to try and strike someone with the ball. Once the ball has been thrown, anyone close enough can pick up the ball and throw it at another player who loses a life if he is hit. It is a rule that to lose a life you must be hit below the knees only, as the older children can hurl the ball with great force. In *Wounded, Dying, Dead,* after one hit they are wounded with two hits they are dying, then on the third strike they are finally dead and out for the remainder of the game.

You must not run or chase when you have the ball or you lose a life.

Over The Rainbow

King Ball

King Ball

AKA: King Ball; Kingy; Dodge Ball; Dodgie Ball; Ball Tig

Action

The game may be started either by forming a circle and having the ball run out through someone's legs, or having everyone gather in a wide circle with their fists towards the centre ready for catching. The ball is thrown to one of the players who has to catch it between their clenched fists, and having caught it, they throw it on to someone else, all the time keeping their fists closed. The ball is fisted around the group until someone drops it and that person becomes **IT**. To save any disputes it is normal to call out the person's name as you throw the ball to them.

The ball must then be bounced ten times to allow the rest time to scatter out, then he hurls the ball towards someone in an attempt to hit them, either between the shoulders and the knees, or only below the knees. Those who are still free are allowed to 'fist' the ball away rather than allow it to hit them, or even pick it up with their fists and roll it out of the striker's way. If someone still has the ball held between their fists, and has not managed to roll it away in time, and a striker manages to tag them, they can be caught this way as well. When a player is struck he becomes a striker and joins **IT** in trying to strike the others with the ball. The strikers are allowed to pass the ball to each other in order to get a better shot at someone, but they are emphatically not allowed to run with the ball. This is a particularly fast moving and exciting game which has the ball 'skiting aboot' all over the place, and is often played within some clearly defined boundary, so that any player running out of bounds is caught and becomes a striker. (You can of course retrieve the ball if it rolls outwith the boundary.)

Finally, the last person remaining free is the winner, or 'King'.

Variations

It should be noted that the name *Dodge Ball* is also commonly used for a much simpler game where a large circle is formed and the kids try to hit a classmate with the ball as he dodges about in the middle. When the person has been hit, whoever struck them becomes the so-called 'middler'.

Dodge Ball can also be played with the players running between two lines, with **IT** in the middle. **IT** throws the ball, while the players run and dodge, to try to hit them. If they are hit they have to join **IT** as hitters. The players cannot be struck if they are behind the lines.

Blind Shot

Sometimes when playing *King Ball,* or *Wounded, Dying, Dead,* arguments can arise. In the event of a disagreement if, for example, a player claims not to have been hit in the defined area, or that the striker took a step before throwing the ball, the dispute is sometimes settled using a 'Blind Shot'. The outie has to face a wall with their arms and legs outstretched, while a striker is blindfolded, steps back several paces then throws the ball 'blind' to try and strike the player.

If he hits them they are out, but if he misses they go free.

'Three and In' Football

Action

This game is played with three people, one in goal and two outfield players. For goals all you need are two jerseys or something similar laid 4 metres apart on the ground. The ball is thrown or kicked out by the goalie and the two outfield players dribble the ball past each other to try to score a goal. The first player to get three goals becomes the goalkeeper for the next game.

This game is perfect for both increasing football skills and stamina, because the more skilful player always wins and gets a rest as goalkeeper and the not so good player is kept outfield doing more and more running so getting fitter all the time. It is a good way to help to even out the standard of play between younger players.

Keepie-Uppie

Action
Another game commonly practised to improve your ball skills is to see how many times you can kick and head the ball without it touching the ground. Of course you can use your chest, knee or side of back heel so long as you do not use your hands or arms.

Rounders

AKA: Glasgow Ringies

'Official' or 'Localised' rules
Officially:
1. There are nine players in each team.
2. Each player bats twice.
3. The bowler must bowl underarm to between about waist and shoulder height on the hitting side of the batter.

Locally:
4. If a fielder catches the ball before it touches the ground, the entire batting team is out.
5. If a fielder catches the ball with one hand after only one bounce then the player who hit the shot is out.

The last two rules are only played in certain parts of the

country.

Action

For this game you will need an old tennis racquet or a bat of nearly any description and a tennis ball or hollow rubber ball of the same size.

Rounders is quite similar to *baseball* and it tends to be played in any large or open area of parkland.

The pitch is formed by a home base and three outfield bases marked out by an item of clothing, hoop, or something similar to form a large square circuit with sides of about 8–12 metres depending on the size and age of the players involved. Two teams of six to twelve players are picked, one to bat, and the other to field and bowl. Decide which team will bat first. The fielding team chooses a bowler who stands about three metres from the home base facing towards the the inside of the square. The bowler throws the ball underarm at between waist and shoulder height over the home base to the first batter. (If the batter is right handed, he would stand in front of the home base and slightly to the left of it in preparation for his strike.) If the ball is bowled to the wrong side of the batter, directly at the batter's body, too high or too low, the batting team's captain will call out 'no ball', and if the others are agreed, another shot is allowed. The batter is allowed up to two good bowls in which to strike the ball.

The fielders spread out to cover the most likely areas into which the ball may be struck, including someone behind the batter to retrieve the ball from any missed strikes. The batter tries to blooter the ball as far out of reach of the fielders as possible, and score a rounder by running round all of the bases and back to the home base to rejoin the batting queue, before the fielders can return the ball to the home base. On the second attempt, if the batter misses the ball, he still has to run, but normally would only get as far as first or second base. Completing the circuit back to home base during a subsequent batter's shot does not count as a rounder.

You are out if a fielder catches the ball you have struck before it hits the ground, or if a fielder touches the ball down on a base that you are attempting to reach. (The fielder must touch that base while holding the ball to put you out.) The game continues until all, or nearly all the batters have been caught or run out and no-one in the batting team is left at the home base. The number of completed rounders is then totted up for that team.

The fielding side now becomes batters and if they beat the other score they win the game. In *Rounders* you are allowed to hit the ball in any direction and very often it can be highly effective for the batter to hit the ball behind him and catch the fielders unawares.

I recall that when I was at school my class got into bother after a window was smashed, and although this had not happened during a game of *Rounders,* the head teacher banned the use of a bat in the playground. Undaunted, the game of *Beezy* or *Beezer,* which uses the open hand instead of a bat, was adopted by the children and it took the place of *Rounders.*

Although there is an official game of *Rounders* with official rules, including the number of bases and pitch size, it is far better to play the way you want to play and enjoy the game.

Kerbie

AKA: Cribbie

Action

This game is really more of a street game, but I do know of schools with suitable unused, private roads. If you can find a street empty of parked cars, that is also quiet and safe, it is a harmless way to pass the time. All that is required is a football of any shape or size. The two players stand one on either side of the street and aim to throw the ball so that it bounces off the opposite kerb. Players take turn about to throw the ball. One point is given if the ball hits the opposite kerb and bounces back towards you and you get a second point if you can catch this rebound before it hits the road.

In some areas, if you manage this catch then you are also allowed a second shot from the middle of the road to score a further one or two points if you are successful. Following this shot your turn is over and the next shot goes to your opponent.

Kerbie

5 *Hitting Games*

Conkers

AKA: Chessies

Conkers is a seasonal game played from late August through until November. Chestnuts are collected in the autumn, and a hole is bored through the nut so that it can be threaded on to a length of strong cord with a knot tied on the end. Some children soak their chessies in vinegar, or roast them in the oven for a while in an attempt to make them harder and stronger.

a conker chain

Action

The players take turn about at hitting each other's chessie (or conker). The idea is to crack open or 'conk' your opponent's conker without damaging your own. You win when you have knocked your opponent's conker right off the string.

Every time your conker wins it becomes more important. One win makes it a 'one-er', two wins a 'two-er', then 'three-er', 'four-er' and so on. Sometimes when strik-

Conkers

ing an opponent's conker the cords get tangled up, and if this happens the first person to yell out 'Strings' or 'Tangles', gets an extra shot.

Long ago, children carried long strings of chessies to school and took great pride in their high scoring conkers. Some conkers were used the following year – these hard, shrivelled (unbreakable!) conkers were called 'yearsies', or 'second years'.

Carly Doddies

AKA: Carldoddy; Soldiers; Rat's Tails

Action

Somewhat more impulsive a game but similar to *Conkers* is the *Carly Doddies;* the name probably originating from 'Carl' meaning a 'husbandsman', and 'Doddipol' meaning a blockhead, although both of these words are now obsolete.

This game uses headed grass such as Meadow Foxtail or Timothy, but ideally you want Ribwort Plantain which is commonly found from May to August growing as weeds on untended grass verges throughout Scotland.

Striking in Carly Doddies

Having chosen two 'weapons' of about 20cm length, the aim is quite simply to take turn about at striking your opponent's stalk up near the head and try to knock the head off your opponent's plantain. The children say with each shot, 'Mary Queen of Scots had her head chopped off'. Usually about ten stalks of Plantain are picked at a time, so that starting with ten each, the game lasts for a reasonable length of time. The winner is the person left holding stalks of plantain when all their opponents' heads have been knocked off.

Shooting Plantain

Action

To shoot the plantain you need to lay the head horizontally over your forefinger, as shown in the illustration, and hold the stalk on to your forefinger with your thumb to keep it held in place. This done, bring the tail end of the stalk up and over the neck to form a loop.

You point the head in the required direction, then pull it as if to pull it through the loop. This makes the head shoot off for quite a distance.

The person who shoots the plantain the furthest is the winner.

Shooting Plantain

Take That!

AKA: Lolly Sticks; Chop Sticks

Nowadays many more children live in towns and cities than live in the countryside, so a more modern version of a hitting game that uses lollipop sticks became particularly popular during the 1960s.

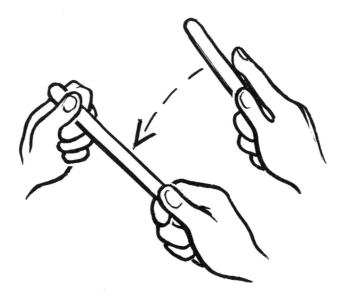

Take That !

Action
The sticks used in this game can either be recycled from finished ice-lollipops (wash them first, otherwise they will be sticky!) or brand new ones can be bought either from craft shops or ice cream vans. Decide who will be allowed to strike first. Striking first is always the preferred option.

The player who is to receive holds his lolly stick horizontally between thumb and forefinger at each end of the stick. The striker holds his stick rather like holding the handle of a hammer but with his forefinger rising up along the top narrow edge of the stick as shown. He strikes his opponent's stick in the centre in an attempt to break it. The players each take turn about to strike, just as in *Conkers*, and play until one stick is fully broken. It is customary to continue with a partly broken stick until it has been completely broken into two separate pieces. However, the partly broken stick must be straightened up again before play is allowed to continue. To straighten up the stick and hold it as shown in the illustration marked X is considered as cheating.

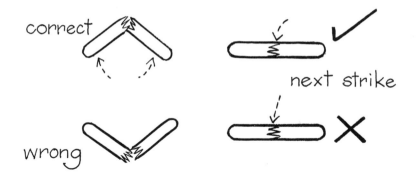

It is also considered to be a case of cheating if the ends of the lolly stick are held very loosely, so that it falls on being struck, as this makes it very difficult for your opponent to have any chance of breaking your stick. It also more difficult to break a wet or damp stick and some children deliberately soak their stick before play perhaps claiming to have just finished their ice lolly. One end of the stick must be dry if this a genuine claim!

The score is recorded on your stick using a pen or

pencil as shown.

If you play this game, please remember to tidy up all the broken sticks into a bin when you have finished playing.

Scoring

In all of these hitting games, the rules can be made such that you can add the score of the one that you have just beaten. For example, if your 'two-er' beats a 'six-er' (and of course you add one because of this win) then this will give you a 'nine-er' as shown:

$$2 \quad + \quad 6 \quad + \quad 1 \quad = \quad 9$$

two-er   six-er   win

Example of a 'nine - er'

6   Racing and Guessing Games

White Horse

AKA: Stookies; Statues; Red Lights; One, Two, Three, Four, Five

Action

Choose someone to be **IT**. The person who is **IT** stands facing towards a wall while the rest of the children move back to the starting line, about ten metres away. The object of the game is to be the first to touch the wall without the person who is **IT** turning around and seeing someone moving. **IT** counts under their breath either very fast or very slow, 'One, two, three, four, five', then suddenly spins around and shouts, 'White Horse' (or 'Stookies', 'Statues', 'Red Lights'). If any child is seen to be moving even a finger, never mind an arm or leg, their name is called out and they have to go back to the starting line. In some versions they only move back three steps. Some children charge to the wall, while others creep stealthily. Either way, the first person to touch the wall is the winner and becomes **IT** for the next game.

Hesitation Starts – Eatables and Drinkables

Eatables and Drinkables is one of the more common forms of *Hesitation Starts* that is played in central Scotland. It is a particularly fast moving, fast thinking game, so if you do not keep your wits about you, the game can be won or lost in an instant.

Action

A 'caller' is selected to stand in the middle between two chosen lines, and at the start, all the contestants gather along one line. The 'caller' will shout out something like, 'Eatables – Bread', and if they correspond everyone races to the other side. First person across becomes the caller for the next round. If the caller had shouted 'Eatables – Coffee', everyone would have to stay put. Otherwise, if they moved they were out. It is also a rule that the last person across is out, so that eventually there should be one winner.

Variation
This game is often called *Odds and Evens* where the 'caller' shouts out Odd, or Even, followed by a number.

Celebrities

AKA: Film Stars

Celebrities is a rather popular guessing game combined with some racing. Traditionally, it was a street game played from one pavement to the other, but has been adapted and is now played between two lines.

Action
A 'caller' is chosen and she stands at one side while the others line up on the other side. The caller will shout out the initials of a well known film star, or celebrity, for example 'W.R.', and everybody in the group starts guessing names. All the funnier if someone shouts out a teacher's or pupil's name that happens to fit these initials. As soon as someone guesses correctly and shouts 'Winona Ryder', the caller races the person to the other line and back in opposite directions. Whoever is first there and back becomes the caller for the next game.

Variation
When someone is trying to guess, they run over and back again *then* shout out the name. It is very amusing because if they are wrong, they have gone to a lot of effort for

nothing! If they guessed correctly they become the new caller.

Polio

Action

A person is chosen to be **IT** and everyone else forms a line about ten metres away from a wall. **IT** stands near the wall and to start the game off he asks for a messenger from the group to join him. He whispers a colour in the messenger's ear and the messenger then returns to the group. He then goes along the group and to each person he whispers the chosen colour and each person whispers back the name of an animal with that colour. This completed, the messenger returns to **IT** and lets **IT** know the names of all the animals suggested, including the messenger's choice of animal. The messenger then returns to join the line.

IT then calls out the name of one of the animals suggested and all of the people who chose that animal run over, shout 'Polio' as they hit the wall, and dash back to the line. **IT** races in the opposite direction and shouts 'Polio' on his return to the wall.

The first one to finish the race is the winner and becomes **IT** for the next game.

Drop Handkerchief

Rhymes

Version A

I sent a letter to my love,
To my love, to my love,
I sent a letter to my love,
And on the way I dropped it.

Drop Handkerchief

Version B

A tiskit, a taskit,
I had a little casket,
I took it to the shops one day,
And on the way I lost it.

Action

A mixed group of ten or more needs to be formed. (I well remember the girls at my school used to go round the playground enlisting suitable (but often reluctant) lads for their game, so that they could start with a large circle of boy-girl-boy-girl all the way round.) Someone is selected to be an 'outie' and everyone else sits in a circle – usually cross-legged, or squatting. The 'outie' – who is holding a hanky – skip-steps around the outside of the circle while everyone sings the rhyme.

On reaching the word 'it' the 'outie' drops the hanky discreetly behind someone's back. A race begins in which the person picks up the hanky, and runs as fast as possible in the opposite direction from the 'outie' around the outside of the circle. The first one to arrive back at the empty place and sit down becomes part of the group and the loser is the 'outie' for the next game. The circle needs to be a decent size so that those racing can wheich round at speed, and have a chance to beat the outie.

Variation

When there is an even number of boys and girls another slightly different game can be played. The girl (or boy) drops the hanky behind a boy (or girl) and they then race in the same direction back towards the empty place. If the girl catches the boy, or vice versa, they have to stand in the middle of the group and give each other a kiss. This version of *Drop Handkerchief* is very funny. If a lass really fancies a lad, they go to great lengths to either slow down or speed up their skip-step during the song so that they can drop the hanky behind a lad they like. She then runs rather half-heartedly so that he is able to catch up with her. However, when the hanky is dropped behind someone particularly undesirable then you will have to do some serious racing. Too bad if you trip and fall!

7 *Skipping*

Skipping is a game that has been enjoyed for as long as the rope has been invented. It is not only a part of our childhood, it has also become a part of our culture and language. Nowadays, we use the expression 'Caw canny' meaning 'Slow down' or 'Take it easy' and this may well be derived from skipping. Skipping is mostly enjoyed by girls, but professional sportsmen like boxers find that skipping is a useful way to increase their leg strength and for generally keeping fit.

You can skip on your own using a short rope, either jumping with both feet together over the rope as it skims the ground, or skip as you run forward stepping one foot at a time through the rope. However, it is great to be sociable, and a lot more fun can be had when you are able to use a long rope and skip with your friends. In one game you can even skip with your short rope inside of a long rope, with the ropes going in the same or even oppo-site directions if you become very skilled. Skipping is very good for you and good for your co-ordination. There are many different games and rhymes of which a few of the more common ones are given here.

Solo Skipping

Rhymes
While skipping a commonly sung song is:

Uncle Wullie went tae France,
Tae teach the ladies hoo tae dance,
First the heel, and then the toe,
Then you do 'Big Burley O'.

Scotland over the centuries has been a deeply religious country and the influence of the Kirk has been far reaching indeed. One of the religious skipping rhymes that may still be heard is:

One, two, three, four, five, six, seven,
All guid children gaun tae Heaven,
When they dee, their sin's forgiven,
One, two, three, four, five, six, seven.

Another not so religious is:

Oh there she goes,
Oh there she goes,
Peerie heels and pointed toes,
Look at her feet, she thinks she's neat,
Black stockings and dirty feet.

Yet another rhyme makes some comment on the rationing that existed during the First and Second World Wars and for some time afterwards:

East, West, ma hame's best,
Nothing like the smell o' ma faither's string vest.
Mither's in the kitchen, rollers in her heid,
Tryin' tae feed a' the weans,
Wi just a slice o' breed.

And would ye credit this one?!

It's the start o' the quarter at the Ro'ness store,
I'm a' rigged oot and my sister's (brother's) got more,
We're baith the bees knees,
And so are a' oor friends,
And oor mithers dinnae pay for it,
Until the quarter ends.

The Bo'ness store was a regional Co-operative Group, one

of the many up and down the country that have now closed or been incorporated into larger groups like Scotmid. The Co-operative movement was extremely important to the workers and credit was freely given on a quarterly basis to regular customers.

The Long Rope With Two Cawing

Keep the Kettle Boiling

AKA: Keep the Pot a-Boiling; Chase the Fox; Follow the Leader; Running Through; Passing By

Rhyme

We're following oor leader,
Set the rope a turning round.
We're following oor leader,
We'll jump in wance and oot we bound.
Dee dum, dee dum, dee dummy dum, dee dum,
Dee dum, dee dum, dee dummy dum, dee dum.

We're following oor leader,
Twice is nice, it is JUST SO.
We're following oor leader,
Nane's cawed oot so on we go.
Dee dum, dee dum, dee dummy dum, dee dum,
Dee dum, dee dum, dee dummy dum, dee dum.

We're following oor leader,
Third shot, we're in another show;
We're following oor leader,
Heel to hunkers, heel to toe.
Dee dum, dee dum, dee dummy dum, dee dum,
Dee dum, dee dum, dee dummy dum, dee dum.

All of the participants in the game chant the rhyme as they jump or caw. For the fourth jump, line four of verse

Keep The Kettle Boiling

1 becomes: *We'll jump in four...;* for the fifth jump, line two of verse 2 becomes: *Five is nicé...;* and for the sixth jump, line two of verse 3 becomes: *Sixth shot....*

Action

First of all choose two people to stand at either end to 'caw' the rope. The rope is set turning, and the girls line up in readiness. The leader then skips once through and out followed by the others so that each girl starts off by running in, one jump, then running out again. On their second shot they run in, jump twice then out again and so on until someone gets 'cawed oot', in which case they take the place of one of the turners. The whole game restarts with one jump and returns to verse 1 of the rhyme.

All in Together

AKA: Call me In

Rhyme

On the mountain stands a lady,
Who she is I do not know,
She has lots of gold and silver,
All she wants is a fine, young beau.
1. So call in my (friend's name) dear...
2. So call in my (Ellen) dear...
3. So call in my (Catherine) dear...
4. So call in my (Maureen) dear...
On the sea shore.

Action

The two people chosen to caw set the rope turning and chant the rhyme to call in each person in turn. At the end of the first verse you have two people jumping in, and the second time around another friend is called in to join the jumpers. The rhyme is repeated with another person called in, and an extra line added with each new verse, until as many people as possible are jumping together. As usual, anyone caught by the rope takes an end and caws.

All In Together

Be my Guest

Rhyme

Vote, vote, vote for (forname, surname),
In comes (friend's forename) *at the door,*
Although she is a guest, she's the one that we like best,
So we don't need (first skipper's forename) *any more.*

Action

One person starts off skipping before being joined by the friend named in line two of the rhyme. On the last line the friend pushes the first skipper out, and this process is repeated over and over until everyone has had a shot of skipping.

Wibble, Wobble...

Rhyme

Jeely on a plate,
Jeely on a plate,
Wibble, wobble,
Wibble, wobble,
Jeely on a plate.

Action

The participants take turns at jumping as the long rope is cawed back and forth across the way to make a snake-like wave, while everyone chants the above rhyme.

You need to be very fast at skipping to avoid being caught by this one!

Rock the Boat

AKA: Rocky

Action

When the rope is cawed back and forth in a low arc it is known as 'Rocking the Boat'. The players in turn enter the rope, jump twice, then leave. If you touch the rope you are out. The rope height is increased for the next shot and so on until only one person remains jumping and is therefore the winner.

Christopher Columbus

Rhyme

Many skipping rhymes use numbers, or the alphabet. One such rhyme that also uses the *Rock the Boat* technique (see above) is:

Christopher Columbus was a very brave man,
He sailed the seven seas in an old tin can,

The waves got higher... HIGHER... and OVER,
5, 10, 15, 20, 25, 30, 35, 40.

Action

At the first word 'higher' the rope is swung half way in one direction and at the next word 'HIGHER' it is both raised up a bit and swung half way in the other direction, and on the word 'OVER', the rope goes fully round again.

Skipping Games with Actions

Cowboy Joe

Rhyme

Cowboy Joe from Mexico, (person skips in)
Hands up, (raise hands)
Stick 'em up, (pretend gun held in hands)
Don't forget to pick 'em up, (pretend to pick up something)
And out you go. (person skips out again)

Cowboy Joe

Action
Everyone lines up, taking it in turns at skipping while performing the actions to the rhyme, then skipping out the other side and returning to the back of the line.

Where's Ma Clothes?

Rhyme
If they're no in the drawer,
They must be on the pulley.
If they're no in the drawer,
They must be on the pulley.
So pu' the pulley doon,
Tak aff the breeks and vest,
Pu' yer breeks up ower yer bum,
An' yer vest doon ower yer chest.

Action
One person skips while chanting the rhyme. For the last two lines you pretend to put on the clothes by pulling both hands first up the way then down the way as you jump.

Following Wee Jeanie

Rhyme
We're following wee Jeanie,
Through the rope then gaun awa,
We're following wee Jeanie,
Next time gie it a faster caw.

Ready noo, we've a' gone through,
Twa... caw faster! not so slow,
And we're richt ahint ye too,
Feet here itchin', rarin' to go.

Action
In many skipping games that use the long rope, with two cawing at either end, the rope speed is gradually increased each time all of the participants successfully complete the rhyme. *Following wee Jeanie* is an example of such a game. Anyone cawed oot by being caught by the rope stays out until the end of the game. As the rope gets faster, the line of people gets shorter and shorter as they drop out, until only the very best skipper is left in at the end. The game ends when all have been cawed oot.

Teddy Bear

Rhyme
Teddy bear, teddy bear, touch the ground,
Teddy bear, teddy bear, turn around,
Teddy bear, teddy bear, show your shoe,
Teddy bear, teddy bear, that will do,
Teddy bear, teddy bear, run upstairs,
Teddy bear, teddy bear, say your prayers,
Teddy bear, teddy bear, blow out the light,
Teddy bear, teddy bear, say goodnight.

Action
This game uses the long rope and allows you to skip for the duration of the rhyme, acting out the parts mentioned. If you are cawed oot you do not take over as a turner, but instead wait until the end of the game. If all of the players successfully get through the rhyme then the rope speed is increased so that everyone is eventually out.

Ma Maw's a Millionaire

Rhyme

This is a particularly Scottish skipping rhyme.

Ma maw's a millionaire,
Blue eyes and curly hair,
Sittin' among the Eskimos,
Playin' a game o' dominoes,
Canny get up tae blaw her nose,
Ma maw's a millionaire.

Action

The person skips normally throughout the singing of the rhyme except for the third line *Sittin' among the Eskimos...* when he squats down on his hunkers doing bunny hops over the rope, then once that is finished he loups up and skips normally again. If that becomes too easy, the fourth line may be bunny-hopped also to make the skipping even more difficult.

Away up North

Rhyme

Away up North,
Away down South,
Away down Alabama,
The sweetest girl I ever met,
Her name was Susie Annie.
I took her to the ball one night,
I sat her on the table,
The table fell, she fell too,
Stuck her nose in the butter,
The butter, the butter,
Yellow, yellow butter,
The table fell,
She fell too,
Stuck her nose in the butter.

Action

In this game the skipper has to go down on her hunkers for the last five lines of the rhyme. It will certainly build up your leg strength and stamina!

* * * *

Very often, these long rope games are concluded by what is jokingly called the *Four Seasons*. Everyone shouts 'Salt, mustard, vinegar, PEPPER!' and the turners caw the rope for a' their worth, as fast as they possibly can, so it becomes quite impossible to skip any more. It is sometimes called a 'peppery' or a 'hottie' when a game is ended in this manner.

* * * *

A traditional skipping rhyme that was commonly used has made a recent comeback since the song has been recorded by *The Singing Kettle*.

I've a laddie in America,
I've a laddie in Dundee
I've a laddie in Australia
An' he's comin' back tae marry me.

First he took me tae America,
Then he took me tae Dundee,
Then he run awa' an' left me,
Wi' three bonnie bairnies on ma knee.

Wan wus sittin' by the fireside
Wan wus sittin' on ma knee,
Wan wus sittin' on the doorstep,
Cryin' 'Daddy, please come back tae me!'

These are only a few suggestions of well known rhymes and songs that have been associated with skipping over the years. If you know a rhyme and it fits your skipping then use it. Perhaps your mum or gran will tell you some more.

8 Clapping and Patting Games

There are a great many traditional rhymes, chants and songs associated with clapping and patting games a few of which I will attempt to explain. The best way to learn one is to ask someone who knows – like another pupil at school – or perhaps your mum may remember if you tell her the words.

Simple Clapping Games

Rhymes
Version A

Clap-a-clap-a handies,
Daddy's comin' home,
Wi' pennies in his pocket,
For his ain wee wean. (pronounced 'wain')

Version B

Clap handies, clap handies,
Till Daddy comes home,
Daddy's got pennies,
But mummy's got none.

Action
You face each other, then take it turn about between clapping your own hands together, then forward to clap palms with your partner.

More Complex Claps

Rhyme
Ma faither went to sea, sea, sea.

Clapping

To see what he could see, see, see,
But all that he could see, see, see,
Was the bottom of the deep blue sea, sea, sea.

Action

T	R	L	TT (each word)
Ma	faither	went to	sea, sea, sea,
To	see what	he could	see, see, see,
But	all that	he could	see, see, see,
Was	the bottom	of the	deep blue sea, sea, sea.

T – clap your own hands together.
TT – clap both your hands, with both your partner's; right to left and left to right.
R – clap your right to their right. ⎫
L – clap your left to their left. ⎭ i.e. diagonally

Ina Spina

Rhyme
Verse A

I went to a Chinese restaurant,
To buy a loaf of bread, bread, bread,
She wrapped it up in a five pound note,
And this is what she said, said, said,

Verse B

My name is Ina Spina,
Come from China,
Do me a favour
PUSH OFF!

Action
Verse A

1a	2	3	1b	2	3	1a	2	3
I	went	to a	Chin	ese	res	taur	ant	...

1b	2	3	1a	2	3	1b	2	3
To	buy	a	loaf	of	bread	bread	bread	...

1a	2	3	1b	2	3	1a	2
She	wrapped	it	up	in a	five	pound	note

3	1b	2	3	1a	2	3	1b
And	this	is	what	she	said	said	said

Verse B

4	5	6	7	4	5	6
My	name	is	In	a	Spi	na

7	4	5	6
Come	from	Chi	na

7	4	5	6
Do	me	a	favour

PUSH OFF!

Verse A
1a) A's left hand is clapped on top of B's right hand.
1b) A's right hand is clapped under B's left hand.
2) Clap with both palms facing your partner's.
3) Both clap your own hands together.

Verse B – Both girls do the same actions
4) Left hand to your right shoulder.
5) Right hand to your left shoulder.
6) Left hand on left hip.
7) Right hand on right hip.
'PUSH OFF' – fold arms across chest and push each other away.

One girl is A and says verse A, while the other is B and says verse B. At the very end of this rhyme when girl B says 'push off' both of the girls fold their arms across their chest (just like the 'oxter breestie' position in *Plainie, Clappie* – see Chapter 4) and bump into each other to push each other forcibly backwards to end the game.

This clapping and action rhyme is really quite easy once you get the hang of it, so do not give up until you have learnt it. When you have mastered it, *show* your friends at school as all of the claps are easier to learn this way.

The Hypnotist

This is another particularly Scottish clap that mentions 'oor ither National drink'.

Rhyme

	Actions
Coca-Cola, Coca-Cola	T, TT, T, TT
Irn-Bru, Irn-Bru,	T, TT, T, TT
Boys have got the muscles,	raise bi-ceps muscle
Teacher's got the brains,	point to head
Girls have got sexy legs,	point to legs
and that's ok.	
I'm gonna hypnotise ya,	cross forearms as does part-
Paralyse ya,	ner and clasp fingers together;
Turn around and faint.	the person chanting turns
	round under partner's arms
	and falls back as if fainting.

Action

For this clap, you simply follow the instructions in the rhyme (**T** – clap your own hands together. **TT** – clap both your hands, with both your partner's; right to left and left to right). It is particularly interesting as it starts off as a clap, develops into doing actions, and ends up with a piece of acting.

Patting Games

The Dusty Bluebells

Rhyme

In and out of the Dusty Bluebells,
In and out of the Dusty Bluebells,
In and out of the Dusty Bluebells,
I am your master.

Pitter, pitter, patter on your shoulders,
Pitter, pitter, patter on your shoulders,
Pitter, pitter, patter on your shoulders,
I am your master.

Action

This is a very popular singing and patting game. Start with ten (or more) people. A leader is chosen and the other nine form a circle with hands joined and arms raised to form arches. The leader skips in and out of the arches in the circle singing the first verse of the rhyme.

When she has finished singing this chorus she stops at the next person and pats them on alternate shoulders while singing the second verse of the rhyme.

The person who has had their shoulders patted leaves the circle and becomes the new leader with the original girl following her in and out of the circle which now has only eight people in it. Together they sing the first verse as they weave in and out of the arches.

This procedure continues, with the circle getting fewer in number and the line of those weaving in and out getting longer and longer, until there is only one person left.

When there is only one girl left she can either lean both of her arms against a wall to form the arch, or often immediately becomes the single leader as the other nine form a circle.

The game ends when they all get fed up or the bell goes for end of break-time.

Dusty Bluebells

The Farmer's in his Den

Rhyme

The farmer's in his den, the farmer's in his den,
Hey o ma daddy o, the farmer's in his den.

The farmer wants a wife, the farmer wants a wife.
Hey o ma daddy o, the farmer wants a wife.

The wife wants a child...

The child wants a dog...

We all pat the dog, we all pat the dog,
Hey o ma daddy o, we all pat the dog.

Action

A group of about ten or more children choose a 'farmer'. They form a circle holding hands and dance sideways around the farmer singing the first verse.

As the second verse is sung the farmer picks a wife to join him and they hold hands in the centre as the group dance.

Then they have a child. Normally a small one from the group but sometimes to be ridiculous the tallest will be chosen. Everyone then sings the third verse, and then the fourth after picking a dog.

As the last verse is sung the children all pat the 'dog' on the head. All but the dog find it most amusing.

9 *Indoor Games for a Dreich Day*

It is not always possible to play outside and unless you are like a duck and particularly like the rain, it is good to know some games that will keep you amused when the weather is particularly bad.

The games described in this section are a smattering of games that have been the delight of many children before you and I hope will keep you amused as well. So much the better if you not only enjoy these games, but they keep you out of trouble with the playground supervisors and teachers!

They have been chosen especially for those days when it is gey dreich and you are at a loss as to what to do with yourself. There is no need to go out and get drookit when you can stay in and have fun with these games.

Penny Football

AKA: Shove Ha' penny

Action

Penny Football is a very absorbing game that can be played at any time indoors. It is often played from end to end of a flat school desk, or on a larger table. Two erasers, or a 15cm ruler can be used to represent the goals.

Having chosen who is to start, any three identical

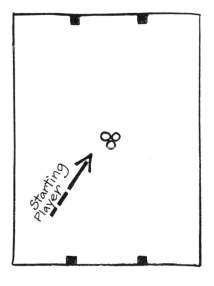

Penny Football

coins are placed in a triangular shape as shown, and the player 'kicks off' by flicking the coin nearest his goal with the fingernail of his forefinger. You must hit another coin with each shot, taking turn about until one of the players creates a suitable gap. If you fail to hit another coin with your shot, then your opponent is awarded a 'free hit' followed by their normal shot which gives your opponent two turns in a row and a golden opportunity to 'break'. The main aim is to try to open up enough of a gap so that when it is your turn, you can try to flick the coin that is nearest your own goal line through this gap at the same time making a new gap that you can shoot through.

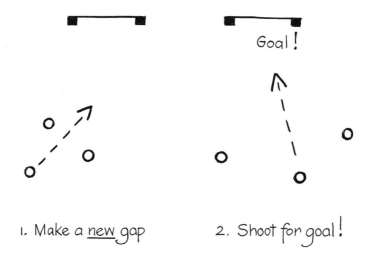

1. Make a new gap   2. Shoot for goal!

If successful, you continue to play until you can flick a coin into your opponent's goal to score and as long as you continue to fire the coin fully through the goal, the 'hit another coin' rule does not apply. However, if you do not manage to strike your coin fully through the gap, and it also has not hit another coin, then the next shot goes to your opponent who also gains a 'free hit' into the bargain.

This has been the source of many a dispute, so to prevent much argument, a ruler or piece of string may be used to measure along the outside edges of the coins. The coin must be fully through for your shot to be correct, and only C shown here is considered as being fully through.

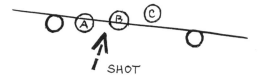

When a coin is accidentally knocked off the edge of the table during your shot, it is returned at the point from where it left the desk into the centre of the table and once again a 'free hit' is gained by your opponent. In some areas the rules require that you must tell your opponent which coin you intend to hit in advance of making your shot, so that if you miss that coin you will be penalised by the free hit rule, even if you were to hit the other coin with that shot.

Once you start playing it is a lot simpler than it sounds. It can be great fun indeed and you can operate a class or school league if you have enough players wanting to compete.

Stone, Paper, Scissors (Rain, Fire)

This game is probably best played by smaller groups of two to three children as a game in itself, but it can be used as a method of choosing IT, or to settle an argument.

Action

The players form a circle or stand facing each other, and on the command of 'One, two, three, DRAW', or simply 'OUT', they simultaneously draw their hands to the centre

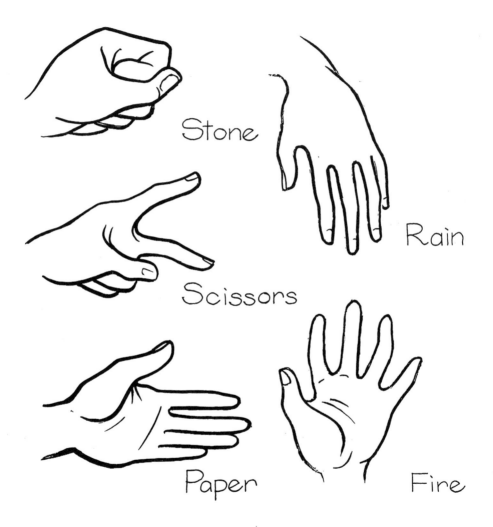

Stone

Rain

Scissors

Paper

Fire

in one of three positions:

Clenched fist – *Stone, or rock*
Two fingers – *Scissors*
Open hand – *Paper*

Stone 'breaks' scissors, scissors 'cut' paper, and paper 'wraps' stone so every one of the choices has a chance of winning.

If both, or all the players involved, draw the same then it is a 'bogie', or 'washout', and they simply draw again. A score is sometimes kept so that the first to ten is the winner.

I worked briefly in the company of a Japanese professor who informed me that this method of choosing is not only common as a game for children in the Far East, but is also very commonly used by adults as a means of settling disputes! It is sometimes referred to as 'chinging' or 'chinging up', and probably originates in the Far East.

Occasionally, two additional positions may be added: rain and fire. Rain 'puts out' fire, 'rusts' scissors and 'soaks' paper, but cannot harm stone, so stone beats rain. Fire 'burns' paper, 'blackens' stone and 'melts' scissors, but of course rain 'puts out' fire. It does get rather complicated to work out the winners from a group when rain and fire are added in, so it is far more common to find the game played with just 'Stone, Paper, Scissors'.

Arm Wrestling

AKA: Elbows

Action

Arm Wrestling is a common indoor game used as a trial of strength between two people. Sit facing each other on chairs pulled up either side of a desk. Place your elbows into the middle of the desk, clasp each other's hands, and lock your forearms together. The aim of the game is to force your opponent's hand down onto the desk. It is normally played right handed, but can also be played left handed.

The winner of this duel is often taken as being the best out of three rounds.

Hangman

Action

This game is particularly suitable for older primary and younger secondary school children. If you can get permission to use a blackboard and chalk, so much the better, otherwise a large sheet of paper will do.

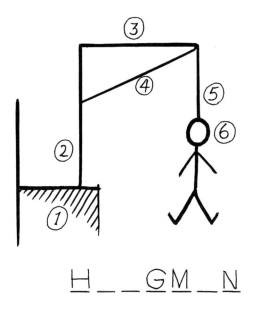

H _ _ G M _ N

The person who is **IT** thinks of a word like *HANGMAN,* then marks a dash for each letter to form a line on the paper. The others take turns at calling out a letter. If they guess correctly the letter is written in above the appropriate dash. However, every time that they guess wrongly a part of the hangman picture is added, first the base, then the vertical beam, followed by the horizontal support, the diagonal cross-member and the rope. Then the figure gets hung; first the head, then the body, each arm and finally each leg.

The aim of the game is to try and find the correct word before you are executed by the hangman.

Fortunes

AKA: Fortune Teller; Chancy; Truth or Dare; Take a Chance

Action

First of all you will need to make a device called a *Fortune Teller.*

How to make a Fortune Teller:
You start with a square piece of paper. An easy way to make a square is to take an A4 sheet and fold it along fold 1 so that the shorter side lies exactly flush with the long side and a sharp corner is made at point C. Cut off the extra section, ADEF, or if you do not have scissors, press firmly along fold 2 then tear off. Re-open the square, ABCD, and fold along fold 3 to mark out the centre, X. Open out to a square again then fold the four corners A, B, C and D back into the centre to make a new smaller square. Turn this small square over and fold the four corners into the centre once again. Fold in half along the dotted lines as shown and firm up the edges by pressing along the length. Lift up and push thumb and forefinger of each hand up into the apex of P, Q and R, S to form the fortune teller. Check that it can be opened and closed freely in both directions, and, if required, firm out any

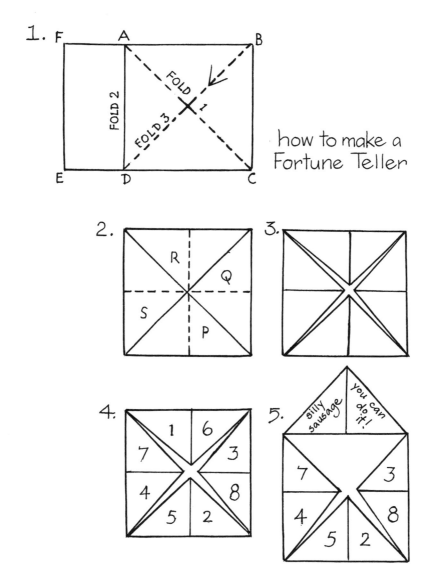

1.

F — A — B
FOLD 2
FOLD 1
FOLD 3
E — D — C

how to make a
Fortune Teller

2.

R
Q
S
P

3.

4.

1 6
7   3
4   8
5 2

5.

silly
sausage
you can
do it!

7   3
4   8
5 2

folds needing slight adjustment. Turn it over and draw in a colour for each of the triangular sections. If you have a good set of crayons and all the right colours you might want to use the 'rainbow' colours, red, orange, yellow, green, blue, indigo and violet which make up the spectrum of white light; leave the last one blank as white. This will help you to remember the colours of the spectrum if you are ever asked at school.

Turn it over again and write the numbers one to eight in a random assortment on the upper sections.

Finally, fold back the numbered sections and on the underside of each number write your message. Nothing too rude, of course, but remember, whatever you write will make or break this as a game.

Well done! You are now ready to play.

Ask your friend to choose a colour. If red is chosen, count and spell out R–E–D, so that for each letter you open out your fortune teller alternately in opposite directions. Ask your friend to choose a number from the four numbers on the inside, and count out the number as before. Finally ask your friend to choose another number and lift up the flap to reveal the message or dare. Read it out to your pal. The sillier your message, the greater the source of the amusement.

Hopscotch

10 *Hopscotch*

AKA: Beds; Beddies; Boxes; Peever; Pickie; Pallies; Pauldies

This game goes back to at least the eighteenth century and for a game to have been played for that long it must be good! As everyone seems to know the name *Hopscotch* throughout the UK, I have used this for the title, but in Scotland the game is far more likely to be called by one of its regional names.

The game can be played either with or without the use of a flat stone or similar object, which in Scotland is most commonly called a 'peever'. A peever that moves particularly well is an old shoe-polish tin filled with dirt; it has the advantage that you can add or remove the dirt until it is just the right weight for your use. Alternatively, a flat stone, slate or piece of tile can also be used. A peever may also be called a 'can', 'tin' or 'box' in your area.

The play area can be scratched with a stone or drawn with chalk on a flat surface (see illustrations). These are commonly referred to as 'beds'. In some playgrounds, beds have been painted ready for play.

Playing with a Peever

Pickie

Action

For this game you will need to draw the *Aeroplane bed.* Boxes such as boxes 2 and 3, that are side by side, are called 'rest boxes' because the player is allowed to put both feet down and so 'rest' one foot in each box. Boxes such as box 1 and box 4 are called 'hoppy boxes' and these single boxes must always be hopped through and

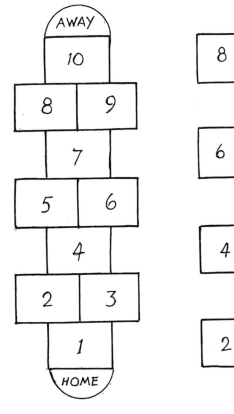

Aeroplane Bed   Totem Pole

out.

Decide on who will start. The first player throws the peever onto box 1. It must land inside the square and not touch the lines, otherwise the 'shot' passes to the next player. Having landed the peever successfully into box 1, the player jumps over this box into boxes 2 and 3 (feet astride), hops onto box 4, then, feet astride, into boxes 5 and 6 and so on going all the way up the bed. The player then turns at the top and heads for 'home'. On the way back the player steps onto 1, picks up the peever and hops into 'home'. Having successfully completed the bed this player is allowed the next shot throwing the peever into box 2, and so on until they are out, after which they will have to wait until their next turn. In this version of the game if your feet touch a line you are out. The players go up and down the bed from 1 to 10, then 10 to 1, and the first player to complete the sequence is the winner.

3	4	9
2	5	8
1	6	7

1	2	9
6	8	3
7	5	1

Square Beds

Kickie

Action

In this game, you can use the *Aeroplane Bed* or a *Square Bed* (see illustrations). The player has to kick the peever from box to box using their hopping foot. It really depends on what size of beds you have as to whether or not it is possible to kick the peever and hop into the next box without letting your foot touch the lines. Very often the rule about your foot touching a line (putting you out) is disregarded because it is difficult enough to find that delicate touch required to hop and kick the peever all the way round. Also, this time there are no rest boxes.

As a general guide, if the boxes are small, disregard the foot touch rule and if they are much bigger, include it.

Advanced Peevers

Action

Some players reach a level at which the basic games described here become relatively easy, so more difficult tasks are added like hopping up and down the *Aeroplane* or *Square* beds with the peever on top of your raised foot, or balanced on your back.

These are really good games for developing your skills of co-ordination, concentration and balance. They can also be played solo, or against other players on almost any flat surface.

Variation

A game called *Ball Beddies* uses the *Aeroplane* or *Square* beds, but involves rolling and stotting an old tennis ball instead of using a peever. Do you know games like this?

Playing Without a Peever – Hoppy all the way

AKA: Hoppy

Action

All of those beds already described can be used just for hopping, but some beds much more specific to this game are illustrated below.

The Totem Pole

This bed can be used for *Hoppy all the way* or sometimes hop, feet astride, hop, feet astride etc. using the blank boxes as the rest boxes for 'feet astride'.

The Line Bed

The simplest bed for *Hoppy* is the *Line Bed* which has the lines much closer together so that the person has to hop sideways up and down the grid.

10
9
8
7
6
5
4
3
2
1

Line
Bed

Snailie Bed

In the *Snailie Bed,* the beds get smaller and smaller, whilst going round in an ever decreasing circle. The game becomes more difficult as the spiral becomes tighter. The player hops to the centre and back out again.

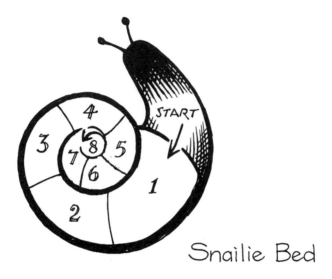

Snailie Bed

TB Bed

The *TB Bed* is another bed in which the lines are drawn closer together so that the player has to hop sideways until they reach the top and can finally rest a foot each in beds T and B. It is not certain as to the origin of the letters T and B. It is possible that they could stand for something simple like 'To' and 'Back', but from its shape and the fact that it is a bed, it is more likely a social comment of the times when the disease tuberculosis was common in the UK and was normally referred to as TB.

Having successfully completed the *TB Bed,* the player can claim one of the boxes in the bed and chalks her initials into this space. The other players have to hop over this space, but the player who has claimed it can use it as a rest space until the game is finished. As always, if you step on a line you are out and the next player takes their turn.

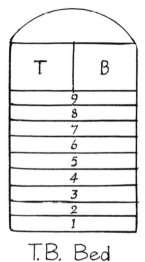

T.B. Bed

11 Bools

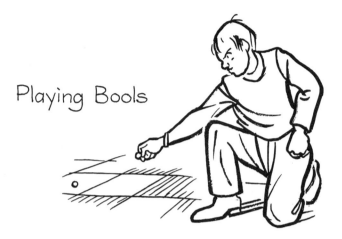

Playing Bools

Introduction

Marbles, or *Bools* as it is more commonly known in Scotland, has been played in its various forms for many centuries. The Scots name *bool* derives from the French word *boule,* which means ball. Marbles has been a very serious business over the years and the expression 'Let's knuckle down to it' meaning 'let's apply ourselves to the job' originally comes from the game of *bools.* There is even an official *British Marbles Board of Control* based in a town called Tinsley Green in Sussex where some veteran enthusiasts still play matches on Good Friday, which is known locally as 'Marbles Day'. In fact, the practice of playing marbles during Lent has been a long standing tradition between two teams of six players using a six foot diameter smooth concrete ring which is raised off the ground. Some fine yellow sand is sieved onto the surface to slow the marbles down a bit. Forty-nine marbles are placed in the middle and the two teams play to see who can knock the most marbles out of the ring. The World Championships have been held at Tinsley Green with teams from as far afield as France, Holland and the USA.

There are so many ways to play marbles; some of the more common games are described here. The games and the names given to the large marble are particularly localised. Marbles can be made of clay, metal, glass or alabaster, and some of the older glass ones are still highly treasured and have become very collectable. Nowadays, there are two sizes of marble: the small ones, and the large one which is normally flicked to hit the smaller ones. Packets containing one large bool and 14 small bools are available in most toy shops.

Early this century, people were relatively poor and marbles were not mass produced to the same extent as they are now, so children had to obtain them from a variety of sources. There were small clay ones, small glass ones in plain or multi-coloured glass, and a large one for 'plunking', but which some kids reserved for throwing. In the poorer families the children would tend to use clay marbles, sometimes called 'dods' made from hard rolled clay, baked in the sun; they would only be able to afford one small glass marble for plunking.

My father describes playing in this fashion. At his country school they also had a much larger marble which he and his mates called the doe. As both this and the smaller clay ones were fawn in colour it is just possible that as he attended a country school in the middle of a sporting estate, these names arose from the terms for mother and baby deer. My father explained, 'Ye couldna 'skite' a doe, so when the school bell went, a' the kids flung the doe as a last resort, and the person who hit the most marbles became the winner; then we all ran into class.' The doe is also the name for the wooden ball used in the game of shinty.

Specific Types of Marble

Bool
General name given to any marble in Scotland, and used in reference to all small marbles.

Commonies; Dods; Commie; Reddie; Clayie
The least-valuable small marble, made from baked clay. Depending on the area that the clay comes from the colour may be reddish brown, brown, fawn, or oatmeal.

Cheenie
A white, glazed china marble.

Dolly; Glassie; Glessie; Goldie
General names for glass marbles which were highly treasured if they were coloured or had colours through them. Nowadays most marbles are of this type.

Cat's Eye
A glass marble, amber in colour.

Green glassie; Jarrybool; Jorrie; Waterloo; Watery
These marbles were obtained by breaking open a very old bottle. These glass spheres were designed as internal neck stops for bottles before modern bottle caps were invented. Their use in the game of marbles varied as they varied in size but generally they would be in between the size of a *commonie* and a *shooter*. *Green glassies* came from green glass bottles, *jorries* could be any colour and *Waterloos* or *Wateries* were clear glass balls.

Glass ball in neck of an old bottle

Steelie
A metal ball-bearing of any size that could be used in bools.

Chuckie; Doe
A large marble reserved for throwing rather than being used in plunking.

Joldie
A large clay marble used as a Taw.

Alley; Bosser; Dabber; Dolder; Doubler; Plunker; Shooter; Taw; Tolley
The large marble used as a Taw, that is, the one plunked to hit other smaller marbles during a game.

Expressions

To dab – hit a gentle shot.

To plunk – to flick the marble used as the shooter.

A Poodle – a little soft flick.

Knuckle down to it – comes originally from playing marbles. The standard playing position is to flick the marble off the inside of the curved forefinger, and an opponent might say 'knuckles down' meaning make sure you have your knuckle on the ground as you flick; it is cheating to move your hand while plunking.

Mosh, Moshie, Moshey, Mooshie – a hollow depression made by revolving one's heel in the ground.

Plunking The Bool

Before you Begin

You will need at least one large marble as your 'shooter' and several smaller marbles, which you can obtain from most toy shops. There is a traditional cotton, jute or leather bag rather like a money purse, with a string that can be tightened round the top and hung from your belt, which is used to store the marbles when not in play. Most toy shops nowadays supply similar bags made from plastic.

Deciding on the Order of Play

Traditionally this is done by a 'nose drop' with the players standing along a line. The players hold the marble under their noses and allow it to drop on to the ground. The person who gets their marble nearest to the line starts, the next marble nearest is second, and so on.

The 'nose drop' is indeed a serious matter and is how the games are started at Tinsley Green.

Ringie

AKA: Ringer; Staikie

Action

In *Ringie* an inner circle of about 30cm diameter is drawn inside an outer 'shooting' circle of about 2m diameter. An easy way to do this is with chalk and a length of string. Keep one end of the string pinned down at the centre, then holding it at the required distances with the chalk at the end, turn the chalk in a sweeping circular motion until both circles have been formed. Likewise, it can also be scratched with a stick on to dirt.

To begin, each player puts three marbles into the inner circle. Having decided the order of play, each player takes turns at plunking their shooter from any point on the outer ring to try to knock some marbles out of the inner

Ringie

circle. If it has been decided to play for keeps, as is normal in this game, then any marble knocked out of the inner circle by your 'shooter' becomes your marble. If not playing for keeps, the marbles gained are held by you and counted at the end of the game. Either way, the player who has knocked out the most marbles wins. This is the simplest form of *Ringie.*

Variation

There are many local variations which add to the basic game of *Ringie.* In one version, an easily identified, coloured marble is placed in the centre of the circle and this must be struck first, with a second shot gained from wherever the shooter has come to rest. The shooter is played from this position in an attempt to knock a marble out of the circle. So long as the player continues to hit a marble with each shot, a further shot is gained, even if no marble has been knocked out of the circle. This continues until the player eventually misses a marble and the turn goes to the next player. In this version the marble placed in the centre is sometimes called the 'ringer'.

Spanny

AKA: Boss and Span; Boss-out

Action

Having chosen who is to start, the first player plunks his marble as far as he pleases. His opponent then uses his set of marbles to try and hit the first marble, or at the very least get close enough to 'span' the distance between the two marbles, by stretching between his thumb and pinkie. The two marbles then have to be flicked together using only thumb and pinkie to complete a win by 'spanny'. It is just too bad if the marble that you flick catches a slope and ends up further away than you could originally span! It can be a 'gey finicky' procedure in a bumpy playground.

Either a direct hit, or a 'span', wins the game so that the players swap places and the victor throws first for the next game. Otherwise the original starting player throws again and again, until he is eventually beaten.

Hen Scrape

Variation

If *Spanny* is played on a dirt track or worn grass areas you are allowed to do a *Hen Scrape.* This involves drawing the sole of your foot backwards along the dirt, in a similar action to that which a hen makes, directly across the line of play so that your opponent cannot have an easy direct shot at your marble.

Many people used to keep hens not so long ago. It is interesting to note here that a different form of hen scrape was also performed in one of the more elaborate versions of peever; the girls gave two scrapes of the foot as they moved the peever on from box number two.

Bombers

AKA: Bombadier

This is not a game in which to use your best marbles in case they get broken.

Action

The best 'bombs' are 'steelies', metal marbles which are often ball bearings of a suitable size. Each player places an agreed number of marbles inside a thirty centimetre diameter circle. The players take turns to hold their 'bombers' at arms length above the ring and 'bomb' the marbles in the ring. Any marble that is knocked out of the ring becomes the property of the successful bombadier, so he will retrieve both this marble and his bomber. As this is a game in which one plays for keeps, if you win one of your pal's highly-prized marbles they are not amused to say the least! They should not be using them in this game anyway. This game became popular both during and after the First and Second World Wars.

Variation

This game can also be played by placing the marbles into a shallow puddle, rather than a circle, if one the right size can be found. The splash caused adds to the excitement, and it is a lot more difficult to bomb a bool out of a dub. In this case the game is called the *Puddley Scories.*

Dirty Pool

AKA: Knockout

Action

Dirty Pool is a game ideally for two to four players. The layout for this game should have five circles, one inside the other, spaced about ten to 20cm apart depending on the type of playing surface. In this game all of the marbles used are the smaller ones (i.e. commonies). It is called

Dirty Pool because if your opponent has a marble on the bull, which scores the maximum of 50, you can try to knock it out with your next shot and make your opponent's marble move to a lesser score. Hopefully your marble will stop on the bull into the bargain. However, if you miss you might end up with less points, or no points at all if you plunk too hard and fire your shot right out the other side of the circle.

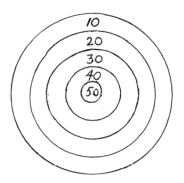

Dirty Pool

Each player shoots five marbles each, taking turn about after each shot, and the one that ends up with the highest score at the end is the winner and claims all the other's marbles. If you are good at this game, you will soon increase the size of your marble collection!

Moshey

Action

Moshey is better known in the West of Scotland. It is normally played on a well worn patch of short grass or a dirt area. Before starting you need to make three indents in the ground using your heel and working each of them in a circular fashion so that you end up with three holes. Each hole is called a 'moshey' and they are normally placed to form the three corners of a triangle with sides of about 40cm length.

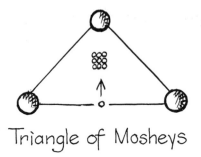

Triangle of Mosheys

Each participant puts three marbles into the middle of the triangle, and from any point along the sides of the triangle you plunk with your shooter to try and hit an opponent's marble into one of the mosheys. Any marble knocked into a moshey is yours to claim and keep.

Variation

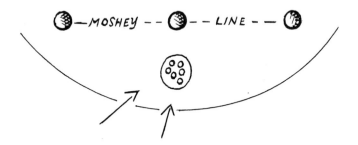

Some people also play using a line of mosheys. In this case you need everyone to put their marbles into a ring some distance back from the line, and a shooting arc is drawn or scratched on the ground. Any marble knocked beyond the line of mosheys, or outside the triangle, should be returned to the centre. The winner is the one who 'mosheyed' the most marbles.

Stankies

Action

Some of the smaller syver covers have little circular holes on the top. In Scotland these metal covers are often called 'stanks'. Roll a bool from an agreed distance on to a stank; the more marbles you can get to land on a hole and stay there until the game ends, the higher your score.

Rebound

Action

This game, for two players, is peculiar to Scotland. You start by placing four marbles in a row tight up against the edge of a wall. A semi-circle is drawn at whatever distance back the children agree upon, and this forms the shooting arc from which the bool should be plunked. All of the marbles used should be small commonies. Any marble dislodged from up against the wall, can be claimed by the successful plunker. For each round, one or two marbles is put in by each player. The score does not matter; this game plays for keeps.

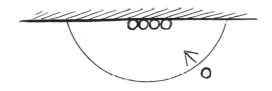

Rebound

Throughout this section I have used the term plunk, but I do know of someone who is certain that he and his pals 'plonked' the bools. Perhaps they were mixed up, or were they just a bunch of plonkers?!

We *plunk* up here in Scotland.

Glossary

This glossary is not intended to give dictionary definitions, but rather to help the reader to understand the meanings of certain words in the context in which they are used throughout this book.

Some of the words are such a joy to use in conversation that I would urge you to help to keep the Scots language alive and try to use some Scots tongue in your everyday speech. Many words sound so descriptive that there really is no direct equivalent to be found in the English dictionary.

Take these words to London and enlighten our friends in the South East as to matters cultural. Given insight and some understanding, I'm sure that they can enjoy a 'guid wee yatter' too!

ahint	*behind*	bogey	*home-made, four-wheel cart that can be steered*
AKA	*also known as*		
awa	*away*		
baccy	*tobacco*	bogie	*game abandoned*
baw, ba'	*ball*	bool	*marble*
bawbee (bawbie)	*half-penny in old currency, (½d)*	box	*one of the numbered beds in Hopscotch*
birl	*to spin*		
blaw	*blow*	break	*continuous run of successful shots*
blind shot	*method of settling dispute in ball game; free shot at someone with thrower being blindfolded*	bull	*centre circle, worth 50 points like in the game of darts*
		bum bee	*bumble bee*
block	*post, or den, used in Hide and Seek games*	burley roond	*to spin around*
		burly, burley	*to spin*
blocked	*to be put out of game by seeker*	burrie	*Bar the Door (Aberdeenshire); to overcome, overpower*
blooter	*to smash, strike with great force*		

119

canny, cannie	*careful, cautious, prudent*	game on	*the parties have decided to play each other*
carl	*husbandsman, working farmer*	gaun tae	*go to*
caw canny	*go, turn carefully; take it easy*	gey	*very, rather*
cawed oot	*caught by skipping rope so out until next round*	gey finicky	*rather difficult to handle, requiring good motor co-ordination*
chap	*to knock*	gie	*give*
chappit oot	*knocked out*	gird	*metal hoop used for rolling*
chessie	*chestnut*		
chookies	*chickens, chicks*	goalie	*goal keeper*
clatter	*very loud rattling noise*	grund	*ground*
		guid	*good*
cleek	*metal hook used to propel a gird*	guile	*cunning*
		hanky	*handkerchief*
conker	*chestnut bored with hole and ready for play*	hauf birl	*half turn around*
		head and tail	*touch on both the head and bottom to enact the catching procedure*
count	*number allocated to count up to in Hide and Seek*		
dee	*die*	het	*IT, he, on*
den	*area that is guarded in Hide and Seek*	home	*starting point/box in Hopscotch*
		hone	*to sharpen*
den keeper	*person who is a seeker, but also guards den*	hunkers	*hams; back of thigh*
		hurl	*to fling, throw violently*
dreich	*dull; slow, tedious, wearisome*	jeely	*jelly*
dribble	*to move ball past another player*	jeely jar	*jam jar*
		jink	*to dodge past*
drookit	*wet; soaked to skin*	jinkin'	*dodging*
dub	*puddle*	jouk	*to duck, or duck underneath*
dunt	*to hit, thump, against something*		
		keek	*to peek*
fair scunnered	*fed up; at the end of your tether*	keg	*a small flask, often used for whisky*
fleck	*speckle; little bit of garment*	kegger	*child holding pretend keg*
form	*bed of hare*	leerie	*act of pulling a leg over a ball as it is bounced*
free hit	*additional shot gained due to opponent's error*		
		loup	*to leap, spring*

lum	*chimney*	scunner	*a bother*
mannie	*IT (Doric)*	shot	*chance to play or*
moshey	*hole in ground used*		*turn at playing*
	in games of	skedaddle	*to scatter out;*
	marbles		*scoot off*
nane	*none*	skiting	*sliding all over the*
noo	*now*	aboot	*place*
nooks	*corners, recesses*	smattering	*hint, or touch of*
o'er	*over*		*something;*
oor	*our*		*superficial*
oot	*out*		*amount*
outie	*runner who is still*	spud	*potato*
	free, or hider not	spudder	*person who counts*
	yet caught		*the 'spuds' in*
oxter	*armpit*		*rhyme*
oxter-	*fold arms in front*	stank	*small syver cover*
breestie	*(right hand under*		*with holes in the*
	left armpit)		*top of it*
peeny,	*apron, pinafore*	stookies	*plaster figures;*
peenie			*shocks of sheaves,*
peerie	*small, pear-shaped*		*like hay, laid to*
	top operated by		*dry in sun*
	yanking a length	stot	*to bounce*
	of cord away from	stotting	*bouncing*
	it; small	stotty	*bouncy*
peever	*flat object used for*	syver, siver	*a drain cover*
	playing Hopscotch	tebaccy	*tobacco*
pinkie	*little finger*	turn	*your chance to*
plunk	*to flick a marble*		*play; a shot*
	off the inside of	wance	*once*
	forefinger using	washout	*game abandoned*
	thumb	wee	*small, little*
plunking	*shooting the*	wheech,	*to draw, raise*
	marble	wheich	
poke	*to prod, usually*	whitewash	*game abandoned*
	with forefinger	yatter	*confused talk,*
pulley	*wooden clothes*		*chattering noise*
	drier suspended	yer	*your*
	from ceiling		
rarin'	*very keen*		
richt	*right*		

Index of Games